The Entrepreneur's Starter Kit

The Entrepreneur's Starter Kit

50 Things to Know before Starting a Business

Paul J. Christopher ▶

an imprint of the American Library Association

HURON STREET PRESS

CHICAGO • 2012

Printed in the United States of America
16 15 14 13 12   5 4 3 2 1

Extensive effort has gone into ensuring the reliability of the information in this book; however, the publisher makes no warranty, express or implied, with respect to the material contained herein.

ISBNs: 978-1-937589-02-8 (paper); 978-1-937589-22-6 (PDF); 978-1-937589-20-2 (ePub); 978-1-937589-21-9 (Kindle).

Library of Congress Cataloging-in-Publication Data
Christopher, Paul J.
  The entrepreneur's starter kit : 50 things to know before starting a business / Paul J. Christopher.
    p. cm.
  Includes bibliographical references and index.
    ISBN 978-1-937589-02-8 (pbk. : alk. paper) 1. New business enterprises. 2. Business planning. 3. Entrepreneurship. I. Title.
  HD62.5.C458 2012
    658.1'1—dc23
                                                    2012003395

Series book design in Liberation Serif, Union, and Soho Gothic by Casey Bayer
Cover image © Konstantin Yolshin/Shutterstock, Inc.

♾ This paper meets the requirements of ANSI/NISO Z39.48-1992 (Permanence of Paper).

For Linda Marie

Contents

Preface

The Entrepreneur's Starter Kit is all about the excitement of going off on your own—being a business owner and entrepreneur. A major theme of this book is "look before you leap." You would not cross a busy street without looking both ways; why would you start a business without a thorough understanding of what you are about to undertake and all the necessary planning tools to ensure your success?

This book was written for anyone who is seriously interested in, or has already taken steps toward, starting a business. You may just be thinking about it, you may have done your homework and started on a business plan, or you may be ready to leave your employer and start out on your own. At whatever stage of the process you find yourself, you will learn (among many topics) the importance of matching your business to your skills and temperament; why planning, including a written business plan, is critical;

and the value of being financially literate. You will gain insights into hiring, marketing, inventory control, billing, and collections.

New business start-ups are so important in these difficult financial times. They offer hope and a solution to those who have been downsized or have limited growth potential with their current employers. Historically, entrepreneurs are the ones who have created the largest number of new jobs and have been the engine for national recovery and economic growth.

Of course, taking the "leap" has risks; this book attempts to be realistic and straightforward about the many issues facing new businesses. Personal and professional excitement always has to be tempered with the cold economic reality the entrepreneur faces. Along that middle path, however, lies the potential for real success.

ONE

Look before You Leap

Things to know before starting a business:

▶ *It isn't easy to make a business successful; if it were, everyone would have given it a try.*

▶ *A business start-up is wrapped in convictions, assumptions, and beliefs, many of which may be false.*

▶ *You can never have enough preparation, and you can never have enough start-up money.*

▶ *True commitment to a start-up business is a lifestyle change, not just a career change.*

A Reality Check

If you are reading this book, you have obviously decided to take the first steps toward being an entrepreneur—meaning that you have chosen a nontraditional path to fame and hoped-for fortune. You are embarking on a program of planning, starting, operating, and worrying over your new business. As best you can, you have taken the necessary steps to ensure your success. Whether you are opening a boutique in a fashionable neighborhood or a consulting business in your home, your decision reflects the same aspirations as literally tens of millions of people worldwide. Basically you are motivated to work for yourself and build a business that you find both intellectually challenging and financially viable.

Your motivation for venturing out on your own may be simple or complex, a mix of events and circumstances, some of which may be beyond your control:

- You have talent that is underutilized and often underappreciated.
- You are absolutely positive you can "build the better mousetrap."
- You have hit the glass ceiling—because of income limitations, lack of career advancement, or sheer boredom.
- You are concerned about long-term security in the job market.
- You need or want a change in lifestyle and work style.
- You can afford to take the financial risk of starting your own business.

A large part of the reality check, and a necessary part of your long-term vision, is understanding, from the beginning, that your expectations may not go the way you thought they would. First and foremost, you must realize that you may fail, and fail badly. From a personal, financial, business, and family point of view, you need to understand clearly that businesses fail—for many reasons. The odds that you will not meet your goals are high, so high in fact, that the U.S. Department of Commerce estimates that 40 percent of all new businesses fail within one year, and of those that do survive, 80 percent will fail within the first five years. Other sources place the failure rate even higher. Imagine these percentages and apply them to the one million businesses started each year—including yours.

What Can Go Wrong?

Plenty. There are countless variables that ultimately affect the success of your business. Some elements are in your control (like keeping inventory levels reasonable), and others are not (a national economic recession). Though all the factors that affect business success cannot possibly be examined in detail in a single book, if you are doing a reality check, it is essential that you consider the following questions.

Just how prepared are you really?

Preparation is the key, both psychologically (you are ready and mature enough to make that leap) and financially (you actually have a plan and some resources). Some people have to act sooner than they had hoped or expected, because of a sudden loss of employment, for instance. Others, out of enthusiasm or overconfidence, act prematurely—they think they are ready but have not sought outside counsel, perhaps not even discussed the idea with a spouse or friend. All they know is that they are "ready" to move; anxiety and irrationality, rather than planning and preparation, are driving the decision.

In some cases being ill prepared may be related to age or work experience. Ironically, some of the most successful entrepreneurs of late have been young technology wizards, but realistically their numbers are few and far between. With age comes more experience and better business judgment. You don't have to spend thirty years in the work environment before you step out on your own, but five or six years of solid management experience in which you gain significant operational and financial know-how can improve your odds for overall success.

Experience is especially important if you move from one field to another. Suppose you have a background in systems and technology but plan to open a retail operation. Working in a retail establishment of some sort will open your eyes to a host of areas that may not have been obvious as you began to plan your business concept. You probably have the experience to make the website for your retail business hum, but do you know anything about inventory control and staffing?

Personal maturity has a lot to do with your future success, whether you are an entrepreneur or in a corporate environment. Look objectively for signs that you need more seasoning before starting off, like these:

finding yourself easily bored
jumping from one idea to another
impatient when learning new areas of business
more concerned about completing work than quality
quick to make important decisions
not following through with promises to customers

    unable to take or follow advice

    overly sensitive when something goes wrong

Age does not have to be a barrier to your business dream. Remember, you can partner with someone who has more experience or seek the advice of a business coach. Both approaches, however, require making a mature decision based on self-knowledge—and this is not easy no matter your age.

Are your personal finances in order?

I devote a whole chapter to this subject, but if you cannot answer firmly right here and now that your finances are in order, or that you have a solid plan to get them in order before starting your business, you should not even be considering starting a business. Keep your day job. It is as simple as that.

Every element of your life—spouse, children, house and all its trappings—makes it harder to leave the ranks of the employed for a life as an entrepreneur. And it takes time to get your financial life in order—not just months, sometimes years. Be realistic: Why put yourself and your family under financial duress when some planning and time to pay down bills and save money before acting will improve yours odds of being a successful business owner? Remember that in life, just as in business, the unexpected can happen; everything from an illness to the loss of your spouse's job can set back your timetable.

Do you have the right motivation?

Closely examining your motivation for going into business is critical to your success. Take the example of a business analyst for a regional communications company. He is paid decently, but he hates his job, dislikes his boss, finds the commute tiring, and gets up every morning wanting to be somewhere else. There are few lateral job opportunities in his area for his skills, so the only solution from his point of view is to start his own company. In fact, he is obsessed with the idea and thinks about nothing else, even to the point of jeopardizing his current employment.

The problem is not the basic motivation; wanting to improve life by owning a business is fine. The problem is that his plan is basically driven by the perception that business ownership is the only solution to his problem. He is not motivated to succeed—only to avoid a frustrating and colorless job. He really needs objective advice from a third party to sort out his feelings and better understand his own motivations. Does he really have the drive to succeed over the long haul? There has to be a stronger, more compelling motivation for starting a business than avoidance.

Is your business potentially undercapitalized?

It is difficult to know if you have sufficient capital. It seems that there is never enough start-up money in a new business once the business has begun. And this is clearly one of the most common problems faced by new business owners. Everything costs more than you planned, and income is much slower to arrive than you expected. You must have reserves to withstand the ever-present gap between costs and income.

Ironically, some people will never start a business because they are risk averse and use the lack of "adequate" capital as an excuse. Cash reserves are never enough for these entrepreneur wannabes. A lifetime goes by without action. The other extreme is the person with debts, mortgages, loans, and a few thousand in the bank who thinks he is ready to go. This is why a business plan is so important and why being in a hurry is the recipe for disaster.

Are you willing to ask for help?

There are volunteer groups, the Service Core of Retired Executives (SCORE), for example, who are willing and eager to assist small business owners. You also have family, friends, and colleagues who are by nature generous and able to assist you with a clear, objective reading of your business plan. People are flattered to be asked and more often happy to assist—with no strings attached. And ask several experienced businesspeople to assist, not just one.

Unfortunately, some budding entrepreneurs simply do not want to rack up billable hours talking to their accountant, lawyer, or business coach. They want to save money; they are convinced that they cannot afford professional advice. Naturally, this is poor economy. If you want to save money, buy used furniture; but ask for and get high-quality advice before you act.

Do you understand all this business about taxes?

The IRS takes a dim view of business owners who do not pay their payroll, withholding, and unemployment taxes, among others. There is no quicker way to get into trouble than to be casual about these matters. If you are a registered company, the tax man expects to hear from you regularly and on time—even if you do not owe money.

Take a lesson from a local retail store that sold upscale wine and fresh-baked goods as a sideline, seemingly prosperous for years in the same city location. Customers found the store shuttered one day with a posted notice from the IRS, which overnight had closed the business and seized all of its assets—including cash, inventory, and the physical store. The owner was served papers stating that his checking, savings, and investments must be forfeited to satisfy an IRS demand for payment. He had paid his vendors, but he had not paid employee withholding taxes or made FICA (Federal Insurance Contributions Act—more commonly known as Social Security and Medicare) payments for months. If the amounts are large enough, the IRS may also consider criminal prosecution, not just fines and interest charges.

If you do not understand these matters, learn about them. The IRS website has everything you need. Most business accounting software also has the core information. You can buy new withholding and tax tables each year. If you still do not understand it, hire a part-time bookkeeper to handle taxes and reporting.

Were You Thinking This?

While you are considering answers to the above questions, be on guard for the following, usually misguided, assumptions many people make as they approach the idea of starting their own business:

One business is like another, right?

Wrong. Businesses share many elements, but the devil is always in the details. A retail store is an entirely different operation than an Internet-based service business. It is essential to know what you don't know. Don't assume that your current skills can be applied to any business; this is arrogant and foolish. Take the time to learn to adapt skills and acquire new skills needed for your chosen business. This is why business coaches recommend that entrepreneurs focus on a business they know something about. Stay close to home; stick to the kinds of businesses that are close to your skill set.

You will learn on the job.

Walking into a new business assuming you can wing it is tantamount to disaster. You may as well take your hard-earned cash and throw it away. If you have researched franchises, no matter what industry they are in, you will see that consistently the keys to success are the mandatory training program and the requirement that a franchisee have management (read business) experience.

The one exception to this rule is a small home-based business, starting part-time with little capital at risk while still holding a full-time position with an employer. You can take your time because you are under no pressure to make a profit and pay yourself to support your family and household. You can make mistakes, experiment with your website, and learn as you go.

You can turn your hobby into your business.

This certainly has happened, and sometimes successfully. But the odds are against you. Try to understand your motivation in this situation. Are you really interested in a business, or do you just want to spend more time with your favorite activities? Are there really enough potential customers to monetize your recreational activity? The IRS takes a dim view of people who insist that their hobby is a business and then take the tax relief offered to a legitimate business.

Everyone will want this!

Famous last words. One of the biggest mistakes is to extrapolate from survey or census data and conclude that the market for your product or services is huge. Most businesses appeal to a specialized market, and even if so-called interested parties run into the millions, it does not mean that you can reach them effectively and cheaply, and it does not mean that they will sign up and buy.

Take the situation of two partners who found the "perfect" property from which to run an upscale garden center. The information they received from the buyer told them that the average family income within three miles in all directions was in excess of $72,000. This seemed ideal, until reality showed them that much of the census tract was made up of young families with one income and one stay-at-home spouse, along with retired people living on fixed income. Even if everyone in the area did like their garden goods and services, many could not afford boutique prices and would instead head for the nearest big box store.

The Internet also fuels this kind of fuzzy thinking by making it appear that everyone is online and therefore a potential customer. If that were true, the art of search optimization and keyword/concept utilization to get customers to your site would not be needed. And even if these potential customers buy, that is no guarantee that they will buy again. Repeat customers are one of the strongest elements in a successful business—and why businesses work so hard for customer loyalty and brand recognition.

You can do it better, faster, and cheaper.

The parallel to "everyone will want this" is the notion that the competition is weak, ineffectual, or technologically backward and you have the better mousetrap. Once operating, you may be surprised how ingrained the competition is, no matter how much you shout that you are better, faster, and cheaper. Buyers are reluctant to make changes if they are generally satisfied—one of the biggest reasons it is so hard to take customers away from competitors. Unless your competition has consistently mangled the customer experience, you will find it very difficult to divert their customers to your products or services. And then you have to deliver to keep those customers happy. And don't think you can do it by price alone. Unrealistic pricing is one of the big reasons small businesses fail.

All this planning is a waste of time.

Why write a business plan? You know what you are going to do. In some cases, you may have been in this business a long time and you have thought of everything. These are, of course, the famous last words of an ill-prepared and unrealistic entrepreneur. Even the tiniest start-up needs a plan. It does not have to be a lengthy, overly formal document. It could be a detailed outline. But if you are going to put money into it or at some point you hope to interest a partner or an investor, and certainly if you plan to go to the bank for a business loan, you must have a proper planning document.

The bank will not give you a loan, so why bother?

If this is your view, then you clearly do not hear the hundreds of commercials sponsored by the banking industry. Not only will they lend money, but many banks participate in programs through the Small Business Administration that back loans to small businesses. Often the banks have little, if any, risk. Having said this, the recent banking crisis may affect availability of funds and interest rates charged. Be prepared to be flexible, and have a strong concept.

Ask friends and colleagues about banking relationships. Visit a bank near your business and talk to a commercial loan officer. Establish a relationship and rapport long before you may need a loan. The obvious start is to open a basic business checking account, make sure that you never go below the prescribed balance, and never, under any circumstances, overdraw the account. Keep in touch by e-mail or another visit or two. Be sensitive about the loan officer's time, but remember that she is in the business of making loans. She wants to add high-quality loans to the bank's portfolio.

Be prepared to sign loan documents that make you personally responsible for loan repayment if the business cannot meet its obligations. The lender wants as much collateral for a business loan as it possibly can get. Never, absolutely never, put up your home or condo as collateral for a loan.

You don't need to be computer-savvy.

In most cases you need the basics to run a business—something like Word, Excel, PowerPoint, and a business accounting software package such as QuickBooks—along with an e-mail application and web browser, plus services such as Skype, Go to Meeting, SurveyMonkey, LinkedIn, and, of course, Facebook and Twitter, to make your communications inexpensive and seamless. If you do not even know how to turn on a computer, keep your day job. If your computer skills are weak, ask your kids, your spouse, your neighbor, or a friend for pointers. Or check out continuing education courses at your local community college. Just be sure to find some avenue for learning the basics.

As your needs change, you will learn more about the software and the Internet systems you use. All software has help screens and technical service help desks. Be careful, though—some charge by the hour, and the costs can run up quickly.

Life will go on as before.

This may be true if your business is part-time. But if your plan is to have an active, sustainable business, this will absolutely not be true.

The reality is that neither time nor money (nor perhaps personal energy) will allow for life to go on as it was. Couples or families may be used to a comfortable summer vacation; you may have to substitute small camping or road trips instead. Plans to improve the house or go back to school may have to be postponed. There typically is not the income to cover extraordinary expenses and fund a start-up business. Something will have to give.

Accept, and discuss with your family, the fact that you will miss baseball games and ballet recitals. Younger children don't distinguish between play time and work time; if mom or dad is around, it's play time. Plan to explain, as best you can, why you are around the house more often or why you are working from home now, and set boundaries for your interactions with them.

When Is a Business a Failure?

It may seem odd to discuss failure before you have even begun. No one starts out to fail. Understanding the word "failure" is important. Much of the data about failure comes from tax records or census information, and in that context a failure is simply a business that disappeared. But a business can be abandoned—no longer needed or wanted—even though it is still viable and productive. Maybe the owner took a full-time job with a large employer; or no longer needed the extra income from the part-time business; or simply did not like the business and the accompanying lifestyle. Someone unemployed might start a service business as a temporary stopgap, knowing that as soon as he finds full-time employment he will return to the corporate world. This often is the case for highly compensated executives, whose vast experience can be parlayed into lucrative temporary service contracts. These executives know that it will take a year, perhaps more, to find similar senior management positions. Thus, not every "failure" is a financial one.

All the same, it is the financial failure that is most common and should be of the greatest concern. Someone's hard-earned money went into starting this business—yours, the bank's, or investors'— and when it shuts down, at the very least, someone has to be paid off. As noted earlier, it basically takes five years before you know that your business is a going concern. Thus, you must enter your new endeavor with a good understanding of financial risks and ways to control them. We address this in detail in later chapters, but one basic and important rule of thumb is to reduce risk at all costs. Unless you are extremely well capitalized, the best strategy is to start slowly, spending as little as possible in the early stages, because it is going to be some time before cash flows with any consistency. In fact, you may find that you never bring in cash with the same consistency as when you received a paycheck.

The first financial rule of new entrepreneurship is to live without:

- ▶ Do without the best and latest iPad, laptop, printer/ scanner, cell phone, and office furniture. What you have now will do for a while.
- ▶ Phone, fax, and e-mail rather than travel when possible. Learn to solve your own computer and e-mail problems rather than calling in a service.
- ▶ If possible, avoid taking on fixed costs such as rent and utilities. If you truly lack viable office space in your home, basement, or garage, look for a short-term lease on a shared office suite or unused space behind or above a retail store as potential low-cost locations.

This list could go on and on, but for the moment its purpose is to set the tone for your business. We will say much more about financial control, personal discipline, and overall strategy as this discussion progresses.

Lost Opportunity

Another kind of risk, often not thought about in the excitement of the moment, is that of *lost opportunity*. Often people begin businesses or buy an existing business because of a sense of impending doom: your industry is doing poorly, your company seems to be on the verge of downsizing or being bought out, and you have real concerns about your job and your future. (It seems contrary, but more businesses are founded during hard economic times than when the economy generally is prospering.)

What many entrepreneurs fail to realize is that not all companies and industries are doomed to decline or eventual failure. Consider IBM, once strictly a manufacturer of typewriters and mainframe computers, which transitioned to PCs and servers and has now morphed into a service company offering business and systems management consulting. There were times when it looked like IBM was in serious trouble, but instead of failing, it changed with the times.

Or examine the history of American automobile manufacturing; several of these companies have come back from the grave more than once, only to emerge stronger and more competitive. Your present company may be in trouble, but it also may have fantastic potential as a downsized and reenergized organization. By leaving your employer and starting your own business, you may miss out on an opportunity to retool or retrain, find a new place in your company or a similar one, weather the storm, and possibly see substantial advancement in your career and salary—including health insurance, bonuses, 401(k) plans, stock options, and other fantastic benefits that larger organizations often provide.

Instead, because you have chosen to go out on your own, you can miss years of full income and benefits, and it will take a hugely successful start-up to make up for all of the salary and perks you might have had if you stayed in the corporate world. Exhibit 1-1 looks at a the case of Kathryn D, a marketing manager of a Fortune 1000 company, and what she could expect in salary, retirement, and other benefits versus what she could expect in the first five years of running her own business. Kathryn had been concerned about her employment situation for some time. Her company is a major manufacturer of industrial coatings, and her main accounts are heavy manufacturers, whose business has been very uneven in the past three years. She searched for other employment, but because she does not have an MBA she found it difficult to get attention from prospective employers.

Her job was eliminated, and thus she did not receive her full salary of $77,000 for that year; instead, she earned $50,000 in 2011 and received a severance of $20,000, making her nearly whole for the year. Because she was well liked and highly respected, Kathryn had substantial contacts within her industry and the local professional marketing association, with which she had been active for the past five years.

In response to her job loss, her strategy was to finish her MBA degree part-time and start her own marketing firm. Rather than continue to look for employment or move to an area with a stronger business environment, she used her $20,000 severance as seed money to set up her company, Marketers Associates, LLC. Her motivation was primarily economic; she and her company had

EXHIBIT 1-1 ▸ **Personal Income: Employment vs. Small Business**

Employment in a Corporate Environment

	2011*	2012	2013	2014	2015	Total
Income/ Expenses						
Salary	$50,000	$82,000	$ 86,000	$ 90,000	$ 96,000	$404,000
Bonus	$ 3,000		$ 1,500	$ 2,000	$ 4,000	
Paid healthcare	$ 3,600	$ 3,300	$ 3,400	$ 3,800	$ 3,800	
Paid retirement	$ 1,800	$ 2,000	$ 2,200	$ 3,000	$ 4,000	
Dollar value of sick leave	$ 2,000	$ 2,400	$ 2,600	$ 2,900	$ 3,700	
Disability insurance	$ 1,200	$ 1,400	$ 1,600	$ 1,800	$ 2,200	
Eye care benefit	$ 1,000	$ 1,200	$ 1,200	$ 1,200	$ 1,300	
Dental benefit	$ 1,000	$ 1,200	$ 1,200	$ 1,200	$ 1,300	
Severance benefits	$20,000					
Paid Social Security	$ 1,500	$ 1,900	$ 2,300	$ 3,000	$ 3,600	
Paid life insurance	$ 800	$ 1,200	$ 1,500	$ 1,700	$ 2,200	
Total Income from Employment	$85,900	$96,600	$103,500	$110,600	$122,100	$518,700

*Assumes lost employment in year 2011

cont.

Exhibit 1-1 (cont.)

Self-Employment in a Small Business

	2011	2012	2013	2014	2015	Total
Business Income	$ 3,500	$36,000	$66,000	$115,000	$250,000	$470,500
Salary	$ 0	$10,000	$30,000	$ 60,000	$100,000	
Rental income	$ 0	$ 1,200	$ 3,600	$ 4,800	$ 6,000	
Dividends/ bonus	$ 0	$ 0	$ 0	$ 0	$ 10,000	
Auto payments						
Share of utilities			$ 500	$ 1,500	$ 2,000	
Company-paid insurances				$ 7,050	$ 7,300	
Company-paid retirement				$ 500	$ 2,500	
Expenses						
Healthcare	($4,400)	($4,500)	($4,700)	$ 0	$ 0	
Retirement contribution	$ 0	($ 200)	($ 500)	($ 2,000)	($ 4,000)	
Disability insurance	($ 500)	($ 550)	($ 550)	$ 0	$ 0	
Eye care	$ 0		($ 200)	$ 0	$ 0	
Dental	$ 0		($ 200)	$ 0	$ 0	
Life insurance	($1,300)	($1,300)	($1,300)	$ 0	$ 0	
Payroll taxes		($1,500)	($6,000)	($12,000)	($22,000)	
Social Security		($ 400)	($1,200)	($ 1,800)	($ 3,000)	
Total Income from Business	($6,200)	$ 2,750	$19,450	$ 58,050	$ 98,800	$172,850

gone through several slow periods, but none as bad as the current environment. Kathryn was convinced that this was the only recourse; she assumed that the industry and her field would be mired economically for years.

But who can predict economic upturns and downturns? This particular downturn was short. Kathryn probably would have found comparable employment the next year, 2012, and her new MBA would allow her to reach a senior-level marketing position and, over the next four years, earn a salary of $96,000 plus benefits, for a total five-year income (with benefits) of $518,700.

Instead, her own business began to grow nicely, but it took until 2014 to really allow Kathryn to pay herself a salary even close to her past income. And it is not until the fifth year that she could fully rationalize compensation and benefits comparable to what she would have made as a marketing manager in a larger firm. Her earnings for the five years as an entrepreneur are $172,850.

There may have been other, positive reasons for starting her company, but these results clearly show that Kathryn would have been financially better off to continue her graduate program and look for employment in the short run rather than try to earn a living from her own business.

Did Kathryn make a bad decision? You have to assume that her personal balance sheet is much less robust after five years of being an entrepreneur; no doubt she used savings and her retirement money to live on while building the business. What is clear is that she got past the so-called five-year stage and that the business showed good growth throughout the period. She seems to have the potential to grow the business, thus justifying the risk and the short-term loss of income.

Many individuals find themselves in similar situations; they are outsourced or have lost their long-term employment, and they think that going into business for themselves or buying a franchise is the solution. It may, in fact, turn out to make matters worse. It is not uncommon that the money from buy-out packages or severance agreements is used to buy a franchise in an industry in which the buyer has little or no experience. Future earnings are much lower than expected and the cost of the franchise is much higher than anticipated, thus leaving someone in middle age in a real bind.

One solution is to test the franchise or new business concept while you are still employed. Chapter 6 covers this subject and the need to plan for small business ownership before you are forced by circumstances to plunge ahead prematurely.

Why Take the Chance? It's Your Life(style)

If the rate of failure is so high, why take the chance? Why plan, look for financing, make personal sacrifices—including financial and lifestyle changes—to start up a business? Many potential business owners would rightly say that with the odds stacked so high it just may not be worth it. Why endure what can be an exhausting and frustrating experience in the best of circumstances, only to see your scheme collapse like a house of cards?

The ultimate reason for taking the chance is that, if you are successful (however you define it), chances are you are going to have the very advantages you are seeking:

> financial independence
> flexibility in work and personal lifestyle
> control over your time and talents
> creative and innovative work environment
> chance to grow personally and professionally

Many people feel strongly that some or all of these results are well worth the risks and costs.

The important thing to recognize is that business is more than making (or losing) money; it is a lifestyle. Consider someone in her early sixties who is planning on retiring from full-time employment in two years. Assuming good health, she has many choices, from volunteering to traveling, but are these all that meaningful to someone who has spent a lifetime accumulating job-related skills and knowledge?

Consider the former school superintendent whose district paid him well and whose state provided a handsome retirement package. His children are grown; his wife is working part-time, and the house is paid for. The family's financial picture is not that of millionaires, but they are secure because of years of careful planning and saving. Is his goal necessarily to make money to pay bills and keep food on the table? Does he have a long-range plan for a business other than the opportunity to improve his income during retirement and keep active and current in his field? The answer to both is probably no. Nevertheless, there is a real entrepreneurial drive behind his decision to build a small consulting and educational practice. In this case, the financial structure and ultimate financial goals may not be the most important part of his decision to write a business plan and start a company; he is likely evaluating his opportunities for success differently now than he would have at an earlier time in his life.

The business is a vehicle to stay in his field, a reason to get up in the morning that is meaningful for him and continues to use his skills and experience. The fact that he can supplement his retirement income is also a plus, but not necessarily the driving factor for being a late-blooming entrepreneur. The superintendent knows that this gig is limited; he wants to retire gradually, and a small consulting business gives him the freedom to work as much or as little for as long as he wants.

If You Still Plan to Go Ahead

Is entrepreneurship for you? Exhibit 1-2 lists assessment questions designed to help you better understand and evaluate your readiness for starting a small business. How many of these questions can you answer "yes" to?

Resources

Small Business Administration

The Small Business Administration has excellent resources that can be used to help you sort through the myriad questions and problems you will face when you are planning a new business. Visit the SBA website (www.sba.gov) and use the navigation bar at the top to locate and click on Starting & Managing a Business. There you will find tools and templates to help you get started.

About.com

The website About.com is a rich resource with several excellent short articles and tips. Use the links on the Starting a Small Business 101 page: http://sbinformation.about.com/od/bizopportunities/a/startup101.htm.

Internal Revenue Service

The IRS has all of the essentials a small-business owner needs to understand and manage tax liabilities. Its page for businesses can

EXHIBIT 1-2 ▸ **Are you ready to start a business?**

Have you ever worked in a business similar to what you are planning to start?

Do you have support for your business from family and friends?

Have you ever taken a course or seminar designed to teach you how to start and manage a small business?

Have you discussed your business idea, business plan, or proposed business with a business coach or counselor, such as a faculty advisor, SCORE counselor, Small Business Development Center counselor or other economic development advisor?

Do you have a family member or relative who owns a business?

Do you consider yourself a leader and self-starter?

Would other people consider you a leader?

Are you willing to invest a significant portion of your savings or net worth to get your business started?

Do you have enough confidence in yourself and your abilities to sustain yourself in business, if or when things get tough?

Do you like to make your own decisions?

Are you prepared, if needed, to temporarily lower your standard of living until your business is firmly established?

Do others turn to you for help in making decisions?

Are you willing to commit long hours to make your business work?

Would others consider you a team player?

Do you have a business plan for the business you are planning to start?

Do you know and understand the components of a business plan?

Do you know what form of legal ownership (sole proprietor, partnership, or corporation) is best for your business?

Do you know why some consider business planning to be the most important factor determining business success?

Do you know if your business will require a special license or permit and how to obtain it?

Do you know how to compute the financial "break-even point" for your business?

Do you know how to compute the start-up costs for your business?

Do you know about the various loan programs that are available from banks in your area and the SBA?

cont.

Exhibit 1-2 (cont.)

Do you understand how a business loan can impact your credit?

Do you know how to prepare and/or interpret a balance sheet, income statement, and cash-flow statement?

Do you know why small business loans are considered more risky than loans made to large businesses?

Are you sure your planned business fills a specific market need?

Do you know your target market?

Do you understand the tax requirements associated with your business?

Do you know how to prepare a marketing strategy for your business?

Do you know how to learn about your business competitors?

Do you understand marketing trends in your business industry?

Do you feel comfortable using a computer or other technology to improve business operations?

Do you have a payroll process planned for your business?

Do you have a customer service strategy in mind or in place?

Do you know how to obtain an EIN (Employer Identification Number) for your business?

Do you know if your business should have some form of intellectual property protection?

Do you know where to obtain information about regulations and compliance requirements that impact your business?

Source: Adapted from U.S. Small Business Administration, http://web.sba .gov/sbtn/sbat/index.cfm?Tool=4

be very useful, especially for starting, operating, and closing a business: www.irs.gov/businesses/index.html. From this page, you can also find information particular to small businesses by clicking on "Small Business/Self-Employed" on the navigation bar at the top.

SCORE

SCORE is a nonprofit associated with the Small Business Administration. Its volunteers offer free business counseling: www.score. org/about-score.

TWO

What Business Is Right for You?

Things to know before starting a business:

▸ *It is critical to match your experience and abilities to the business you want to start or buy.*

▸ *There are a variety of risks that come with every business; understanding these risks is basic to your decision making.*

▸ *Starting a business is on a risk/reward continuum, just like buying stocks or bonds.*

▸ *Knowing the pros and cons of buying a business versus starting a new one is critical.*

▸ *The library is a great place to start your life as an entrepreneur.*

Self-Examination

You know that you want to own your own business; the question is, what kind? What kind of business is suited to your talents, education, and experience? This is by far the most difficult and the most important issue you will face before venturing off. Consider some of the general variables that come into play:

> ▸ Are you good at starting and planning, or should you consider buying an existing business?
> ▸ If buying a business, are you attracted to a franchise or a privately held company?
> ▸ Is your goal to own a service business or a manufacturing/distribution company?
> ▸ Do you want a retail business?
> ▸ Do you plan to work part-time, full-time, or start part-time and then grow to full-time employment/ management?
> ▸ Is business growth important, or are you satisfied with a smaller, more contained business concept?
> ▸ Do you have or need partners, either for their financial backing or for their business acumen and skills?
> ▸ What skills and background do you bring to the business? Marketing? Management? Financial? Technological?
> ▸ How much can you afford to invest to buy or start a business?

Naturally, this is just the start of this process.

Self-examination is never easy. Throughout this book you are asked to evaluate your skills and potential performance based on a myriad of factors and circumstances—many of which you cannot anticipate. How do you know what your reaction is going to be when your first important marketing campaign fizzles or when you have more business than you can manage or even think about. These are both extremes, of course. Nevertheless, spending time visualizing what you expect to happen and then anticipating your ability to respond is essential for being both a good manager and a good entrepreneur.

Successful entrepreneurs have given time to anticipate how they want their business to look and how they want it to be. Intention is a powerful and dynamic tool. If you are not inclined toward intention and visualization, talk to successful athletes and you will discover that, before each competition, they try to envision exactly how they want things to turn out. Imagine what it will feel like when you reach a particular set of goals. Get in touch with the feelings you would have as a successful entrepreneur. Practice and conceive of the sense of empowerment and the joy of having succeeded.

If you were to investigate franchising, you would quickly learn that franchisors value buyers who have general business experience, especially experience that is very similar to the franchise to be purchased. Franchisors make money only if they select and sell franchises to individuals whom they judge to have the right stuff— the potential to manage the business as taught by the franchisors and to handle problems literally by the book. In fact, franchisors often can be rather rigid and will pull franchises from owners who are not operating as they have been taught and as customers have come to expect. In effect, you rent a franchise and continue to work and profit only if you are trained and follow the training and the franchise concept. The end result is that franchisors are looking for a certain type of person: someone who can follow the program and execute according to the franchise model. They are not looking for free thinkers—people who open their business at odd hours or offer discounts when they feel like it.

What does this tell you about the franchisor selection process, and what does it tell you about your process when you evaluate the prospects of taking on a franchise or starting your own business outside of the franchise model? The single most important factor is matching the individual with the business concept.

The Right Match

What is it in your personal background, education, or work experience that will enhance your prospects for success? What management, financial, organizational, and selling skills do you have that can be parlayed into a successful business operation? What is it about your business concept that is uniquely suited to you? What weaknesses or lack of experience do you have that must be overcome before you can be successful in your new business?

Think long and hard, because this is not an easy task; few people can be and are objective about their skills and abilities. Some people gloss over glaring deficiencies in their work ethic and skills; others routinely underestimate the value of their experience. How do you strike a middle ground that will truly help you judge your background as well as personal and professional experiences in such a way that they represent an objective as possible scorecard to use to prepare for your business decision.

In a variety of books and other literature on business start-ups, writers like to try to describe the prototypical entrepreneur. They use words like *bold, independent, creative, visionary, risk-taker, resourceful, adaptable,* and a host of other traits—which may or may not be true about any real entrepreneur. More important than such characteristics, when evaluating your ability and willingness to take on a business start-up you need to focus on behavior or skill sets—those bits of learned behavior, from either experience or formal education and training—that will assist you in starting, operating, and profiting from your business.

Consider some of the following skill sets when making a self-evaluation in anticipation of starting a business. More than likely, you will find yourself on one side of each pair or the other:

a good generalist, jack-of-all-trades

a good specialist, can manage one or two parts of the
    business very well

a doer, likes to be hands-on in all areas

a manager, likes to know generally but prefers to delegate

an idea person, creative and clever with unusual responses to
    situations

an implementer, can follow the book and manage a process
    specifically

a big-picture person, can plan and see how all the parts fit
    together

a detailer, very good at the specifics

a seller, enjoys the challenge of communication and
    persuasion

a handler, works behind the scenes to make sure everything
    is completed

a finance guru, loves the details

a finance nerd, hates the details and just wants the conclusion

the communicator, can write with ease and speak before a
    group
the reserved individual, hates to write and would rather not
    speak before a group

the planner, good at building and following plans
the spontaneous, can go with the flow

Even though you have only one side of a pair, you can match up with someone else and combine your skill sets. For example, even if you are not a seller, you can hire someone who is or find a partner who likes nothing better than the challenge of making the difficult sale. The point is to recognize those behaviors you have and those you need—from employees, partners, advisors (lawyer, coach, accountant), or even your spouse.

All entrepreneurs must be problem solvers; if you cannot face the challenge of solving business and management problems, almost on a daily basis, you probably should not venture out on your own. You don't have to be able to solve everything—but you do need to know where to get the assistance when you can't deal with something yourself. You may be a decent computer geek, but there will be times when you have to bite the bullet, spend the money, and call in professional help. Being slightly stubborn is a good behavior set, but being stupidly stubborn and unwilling to admit that you need help is another matter entirely.

During the course of your self-evaluation, ask yourself if you are grounded in reality. Can you really understand the complexity and the difficulty of the task you are taking on? Can you grasp, at least reasonably so, the levels of personal and financial risk you are about to take?

Whatever kind of business you plan for, you must go into it with a sense of urgency and a good deal of self-confidence. Who is going

---

Realistic Expectations

A recent ten-year study by an international consulting firm revealed that one of the major reasons small businesses fail is that "the business quits before it gives itself sufficient time to succeed." Many business owners walk into the situation expecting instant success, and when that does not happen they become unhappy, stressed, and dissatisfied. "Expecting an immediate return on any investment is not realistic and makes for an unhappy and unproductive business owner."

---

to believe you, invest in you, trust you—become an employee or a vendor—if they are not confident about your commitment and your business skills? Just saying everything will work out doesn't make it so. Wishing is not doing, and the other stakeholders in your business will look for a leader who is grounded in reality. Vendors and customers do not want to hear pipe dreams or get a sense that somehow the business will run itself. They want to deal with a person who has a vision, but with feet on the ground. Entrepreneurs have confidence in themselves and in their ideas. Most of all, they are willing to invest the time and energy and money to make it all work.

Willingness to Stick It Out

Being grounded means that you understand that a business does not turn on a dime. It takes time, and the willingness and ability to stick to it are extremely important. The fact is, it takes time to build a business, for a reputation to be established, for customers to know you, and for vendors to trust you. It takes time to write a business plan, to modify that plan, and to implement that plan (and then to modify it again, as often as needed). It takes a day just to get the cable guy out to connect your Internet service.

A willingness to stick it out means that you are sufficiently a risk taker, that unless obvious disaster hits, you can see a future for yourself in your chosen business and will devote the energy to slowly lay the foundation for your success. It also means a willingness to make sacrifices—personal, social, and financial.

The kind of business you choose, with which you feel most comfortable, will be one that can be supported by your lifestyle and your finances. Starting a small Internet-based business is a great deal easier on the pocketbook and your psyche than making a five-million-dollar offer for a small restaurant chain—open 24 hours a day, seven days a week. Both have a degree of risk; both require grounding and commitment. But the latter is an expensive, aggressive plan. Can you support such a venture emotionally and psychologically—or any one of hundreds of ideas that may require more financial and psychological resources than you can come up with?

A key component for any entrepreneurial drive is the support system. A spouse and family not fully committed to the new venture are a recipe for disaster. Without being told, they know that they may have to sacrifice to help ensure the business's success. This may not be a commitment everyone is willing to make. A great deal will change:

   working out of the house
   less vacation and family time
   postponing major purchases such as a new house or car
   longer working hours
   restrictions on use of part of the home space for an office
   personal as well as financial stress

Because the value proposition of owning your own business is so high, the appeal to many people so strong, there can be a compulsion to act—to make decisions before all the support mechanisms are in place. Enthusiasm directs individuals to want to move quickly, responding to perception that an opportunity will be lost. Don't let that sway you. Caution and thoughtful prudence should always rule the day. There will always be more deals, more opportunities, and a host of business choices. Don't let others convince you that you must act now. You are being hustled—just as when the used car salesman tells you that this is the only vehicle like this on the lot at this price. *Indeed*, you say—and you should. Resist the pressure to act hastily.

Your ability to go the extra mile, to stick it out until the business matures and is financially sound, is strongly influenced by other support groups as well, such as partners or investors (active or passive), relatives and friends, former colleagues and business contacts, a business coach, accountants and bankers, lawyers, and tech consultants. Each support group has a different function. Accountants and lawyers serve unique roles and their expertise may be infrequent; they will, however, inevitably be critical to your success. A business coach or your spouse may be your ultimate support personnel, since she will listen, observe, advise, counsel, and otherwise encourage you in your everyday endeavors.

Starting a business is something like going to war. It seems like a good idea at the time: bands play, politicians give speeches, promises of a short fight are made, zeal and patriotism are high. Of course, wars are never short and never without sacrifice of personnel and treasure. The longer the war goes on, the more difficult it becomes. You open your business with a reception, an announcement in the paper, mailings to all of your friends and colleagues; you are greeted with kindness, enthusiasm, and encouragement. Weeks later the phone calls stop, the cards, letters, and e-mails cease, and it is now the daily grind of trying to build a business. The war is on.

Risk and Reward

When you are trying to determine the kind of business best for you and your circumstances, know that you will always take on some risk. What is important is that the risk be in some proportion to the future reward. Consider a stock market investor who buys a company's shares at a very high price; he does so with the expectation that he has paid a premium because he is sure that there is very little risk from the investment.

Your future business should be evaluated in much the same way. If your expectations are that you will gain $500 a month in extra income, your risk expectations should be rather low. If, on the other hand, you have expectations of starting or buying a substantial business that will provide long-term security over your lifetime, your risk/reward ratio will be much higher and very different. Business owners get into a great deal of trouble when they invest heavily, taking on debt or a second mortgage for a house, and the business proposition is either out of balance because of potential future revenue (e.g., you paid too much for the business) or it is a bad business model with little chance of success (it should have been bought for a bargain price, not at a premium).

Risks can come in many forms. Naturally and obviously, there is *financial risk:* you invest and your business fails and you lose your capital. But you may have lost more than that: You may be up to your ears in debt with bank loans and credit card advances. You may even have lost your house because it was used as security for the business. You may ultimately file for bankruptcy and must start again—without a full-time job, adding insult to injury.

There is also *economic risk:* You have an excellent concept, a well thought-out plan, financial backing, and the professional expertise to be successful, but the overall economy falls into recession. Money from lenders or investors disappears overnight as both groups become more conservative. Vendors you had counted on demand payment up front or put limits on your credit line. Customers you had counted on are buying less or are overly price-sensitive. Suddenly you are constrained by events over which you have no control.

There is always *interest rate risk:* you are the least likely to get high credit limits and good rates because you are the most likely to fail. (Bankers, too, understand risk and reward and will lend to new ventures only if they are assured of a premium on their loans.) If your new company is capital intensive, that is, requires large purchases in inventory, equipment, or personnel, small increases in interest charges can be like a cancer on the business—slowly eroding net profit and cash flow. Once interest rates go up, they tend to move quickly; just as predictably, they tend to go down very slowly as banks and financial institutions attempt to recover lost profits from bad loans. As a business owner, you have little choice but to accept and anticipate interest rate changes. As a borrower, you can do nothing to change this cycle—only avoid it by not borrowing at all, using your assets and other people's money ("OPM"). You may not have a source of investment capital available, so borrowing may be your only recourse to fund the business.

There is also *marketing risk,* which can be an odd assortment of outside events that you cannot control either: product obsolescence (particularly in high-tech and consumer products); better or cheaper product launched by a competitor; loss of a major distributor; loss of key (hard-to-replace) personnel; and delays in product launch. Some marketing risks you may be able to control—within limits. Others, such as an unexpected resignation of key personnel, you cannot control.

Operational risks are the easiest to control and anticipate, but that does not mean that they are not out there and that they cannot bring a business down. A dishonest partner or embezzling employee; a supplier who goes out of business; a warehouse fire; a catastrophic computer failure—these are just some of the kinds of operational risks that can destroy a business. Good internal controls, adequate follow-up on problems, and vigilance may ultimately reduce these kinds of risks.

Capitalization risk is one of the most difficult problems for new businesses. Even though you are grounded, even though you wrote and rewrote your business plan, even through you did a thorough analysis of cash needs in years one and two, you find yourself undercapitalized—unable to hire and train employees, cutting the marketing budget, not paying yourself a salary (or for that matter reimbursing yourself for ordinary business expenses), and unable to pay basic bills on time. This is frustrating because you felt you had the numbers down pat—with a cushion to spare. Everything costs more, and there are always unanticipated expenses, some of which can be substantial.

Undercapitalization is so stressful that only business owners with iron resolve do not give in to the pressures. And, of course, the more you need the cash, the harder it is to find the cash. Bank lines of credit are maxed out and the banker says no to any additional funds. Investors look at your income and cash flow statements and see only red and turn you down for investment. Your spouse, family, and supporters are sure that putting additional money into the business is a bad idea—their view is to cut your losses, get a day job, and try to dig yourself out over the next ten years.

Finally, include *management risk*—the risk that you, your staff, or your partners simply lack the skills or expertise to pull it off. Of particular concern is you as the leader/owner/founder and whether you have the necessary skill sets to management business functionally. Small businesses, by definition, fall short in depth of management—it may be only you, not a full staff of departmental experts. Can you make up for this structural deficiency? Thus the discussion comes full circle: matching background and experience with the type and kind of business you wish to own.

Business Models

Businesses are often classified into two types: those that service other businesses and those that sell to consumers. There are certainly businesses that sell to both consumers and other businesses— many technology and computer companies, for example. But to serve both consumers and other businesses requires a complicated model, one typically seen only in larger, mature businesses that have the financial, marketing, and technical resources to do business in two very different worlds. In this book, we do not discuss this type of business at length.

A business can sell products or services or both products and services. A retail appliance store not only sells new washers and dryers but generates a great deal of money servicing customers who have purchased in the past. In this case the service side supports the product side, but it may well be as profitable (or more so) than selling new appliances. Car dealers do the same. They spend a great of money advertising to bring you back to them to get your oil changed and have other repairs made. This is what generates their profits; markups on car sales are rather small.

There are three basic ways (besides inheriting a business from your grandfather) to actually acquire a business. You can go the franchise route; you can buy an existing business, including franchises that are already in operation; or you can start a business from scratch. All three have financial advantages and disadvantages, and all three require serious planning, oversight, and hard work—using the tools, techniques, and insights provided in this book. Much of this book is devoted to starting a business from scratch. In this section, we focus on the other two options—investing in a franchise and buying an existing business—to aid the process of determining what kind of a business owner you are most suited to become.

Franchising

A franchise is a legal and commercial relationship between the owner of a trademark, service mark, trade name, or advertising symbol and an individual or group wishing to use that identification in a business. The franchise governs the method of conducting business between the two parties. Generally, a franchisee sells goods or services supplied by the franchisor or that meet the franchisor's standards of quality.

Franchising is based on mutual trust between franchisor and franchisee. The franchisor provides the business expertise (marketing plans, management guidance, financing assistance, site location, training, etc.) that otherwise would not be available to the franchisee. The franchisee brings the entrepreneurial spirit and drive necessary to make the franchise a success.

There are primarily two forms of franchising: product/trade name franchising and business format franchising. In the simplest form, a franchisor owns the right to the name or trademark and sells that right to a franchisee. This is known as *product/trade name franchising.* For example, a Toyota dealership or Pepsi-Cola bottling are examples; the owners structure their operations to their own strategy rather than have a franchise that insists on a prescribed strategic and operational standard. The more complex form, *business format franchising,* involves a broader ongoing relationship between the two parties. Business format franchises often provide a full range of services, including site selection, training, product supply, marketing plans, and even assistance in obtaining financing. Common examples are Wendy's, Jiffy Lube, and Seven-Eleven. The franchisor is active in the business, especially sales and marketing support, and provides operational specifications the franchisee is expected to follow.

Many new small-business owners choose franchising over starting a new business because it provides easy access to an established product, reduces many of the risks involved in opening a new business, provides access to proven marketing methods, and in some instances provides assistance in obtaining start-up capital from financing sources. There are advantages and disadvantages, and sometimes it is a toss-up:

ADVANTAGES

> established product or service, often a national reputation
> lower failure rate
> buying power
> may provide some initial financing

DISADVANTAGES

> high start-up costs for popular franchises
> ongoing royalties to be paid
> ongoing support not always as good as advertised
> inexpensive franchise often has much higher risk
> franchise may be difficult to sell

MAYBE, MAYBE NOT

> technical and managerial assistance, but high service costs
> quality control standards, but it is their way or the highway

Essentially you buy the right to sell the company's goods and services within a certain geographic area, using its branded products, under its general marketing umbrella—for which you pay start-up fees, training fees, and a percentage of gross profits (sales less the cost of goods sold). Though you are your own boss, you in fact work for the franchisor. You cannot limit, change, alter, or otherwise make substitutions in the product line, the store presentation, the services offered, or the goods sold. You have some freedom to set office, store, and working hours; to hire employees; and generally to direct the tone and style of the business. In the end, if you violate the franchise agreement, you can lose your business—because in reality you are leasing a business.

Deciding whether to take on a franchise is no easy matter. There is no doubt that those who have gone this route often are very successful and very satisfied. You need only look around you to see major food retail expansion to the four corners of the earth. Still, you need a great deal of information before choosing a franchise. The best advice is to get advice; don't sign something you don't understand; work with franchises that have a strong, hands-on approach with their franchisees, and most of all be realistic about what you are getting into. Like any business, it requires hard work, dedication, and long hours. There are no shortcuts.

Buying a Business

Buying an existing business has some of the same benefits as franchising in that there is an established company with a brand and a market presence. If the company is profitable, it will be expensive unless you can arrange some gradual earn-out as a means of buying the owners out over time. Most small businesses are privately held, meaning that they are not owned by stockholders (i.e., publicly held). Therefore, they do not have the same strict accounting rules and regulations that public companies have, which means that you must look hard at what you might be buying. Due diligence—this is you making sure that all the information you are provided by the owners is accurate—is most important. You do not want to take over a company and then find a drawer full of unpaid bills that are 90 days past due. Owners can have some very "creative" ways of running their businesses, including keeping records; the only real controls on them are the IRS (even then there is a very small chance of them being audited) and bank auditors (assuming they have a line of credit with the bank).

Buying an existing business, then, means that you have to find out what is actually going on as opposed to what appears to be going on. This does not assume anything illegal or unethical—but the company may not be using the best and most current business practices; or the financial officer and accountant may have a way of doing things that is not necessarily standard. Look for overstated revenues, off-the-books payments to owners and family members, guarantees for personal loans, excess inventory, and a host of similar practices.

Having said all of this, there can be some real advantages to buying a business, especially if you can buy out ownership over time. If the current owner is willing to work part-time for a year or two after the sale, there is greater continuity in the business—you get to know the customers, vendors, employees, bankers, and other stakeholders and build your own relationships. Some privately held businesses can be purchased relatively cheaply, especially if they do not have large amounts of assets on the books—buildings, inventory, equipment, and vehicles, for example. A service business, such as a hair salon, has some equipment and maybe a lease, but its main asset is its location and customer base, along with its goodwill.

You might find a business that has fallen on hard times, and it is in part of the business world that you happen to understand. This can be a golden opportunity to fulfill your dream of being your own boss at a reasonable price. Your planning and decision making, however, need to focus on what it might take to turn the business around. Assume that it is going to take longer, cost more, and be more difficult than you first imagined. There are both structural and economic reasons why this business is failing. You may be able to cure some of the problems, but not all. Tread carefully and use every personal and professional resource at hand to guide your decision.

Although most businesses are for profit, some are chartered as not-for-profit companies. One example might be a day care. That they are incorporated as not-for-profit does not mean that these businesses cannot make a small profit. Tax rules may limit profitability, but they certainly can be successful, cash-generating businesses that can pay owners and employees good salaries and benefits. Speak to your advisors before making this kind of decision.

Just as when you are buying a house, there are brokers for businesses as well. In fact there is a whole industry centered on buying and selling small- to medium-size businesses. Find the players, make appointments, get to know them; learn what criteria sellers look for in buyers, what kind of financing you must have in place—and a thousand other details. You or the seller or both will pay a commission for these services, but it may well be worth the cost. A good business broker can lead you to companies or businesses you may have never considered. Brokers can open some important doors.

Finding Your Business Style

The big question is to decide what type of business or combination of business styles fits your vision and your skill set. Use exhibit 2-1 to make some relative judgments about the kind of business best suited to your experience and skill set. Place a check mark in the box that best reflects your preferences as a means of narrowing down your choices.

EXHIBIT 2-1 ▸ **Business Type Grid**

	Business to Business	Business to Consumer	Business to Business and Consumer
Franchise			
Start from Scratch			
Buy a Business			
Service Business			
Manufacturing/ Distribution			
Internet			
Retail			
Direct Mail			
For-Profit			
Not-for-Profit			

Many would-be business owners have one idea and one idea only of what they want their business to be. They have dreamed of this concept for years, nurtured it, and never stopped to examine it in light of other entrepreneurial plans or concepts. Two of the classic examples are opening a small restaurant or a bed-and-breakfast. Over time, the dreams become idealized—the planner sees only success and great personal satisfaction. This person likes to cook, likes people—why wouldn't he be great in a restaurant setting? Or think how much fun it would be to retire to a resort area, buy the big house, and supplement retirement income with a bed-and-breakfast.

Well, thousands before you have had similar dreams, and thousands before you have failed or quit these kinds of businesses because they are tremendously difficult to manage over the long haul. Both of these businesses require long hours, with razor-thin margins. Just look around at the number of eating establishments that open and then close within a year or two—and these are people who work in the industry. Can you make a go of your dream business? Of course you can. But open yourself to all kinds of possible business opportunities. Don't decide ahead of time what industry or which kind of business you should own. Learn, study, evaluate, seek advice—but most of all, be open to possibilities that may arise.

As a general rule, a service business is much easier to start than one that involves manufacturing or distribution. The cost of entry is cheaper because many fewer assets are required to generate income. A service model can be started part-time in your home—further reducing costs. The problem may be that there are literally tens of thousands of these kinds of businesses being formed around the world every month. Like any business concept, finding the one that clicks is difficult and requires a good deal of creativity and research.

If your business is a manufacturing or distribution company, the costs to enter certain markets can be prohibitive. If a product is the focus of your business, consider jobbing out the manufacturing; go overseas or to a local group that can produce products to your specifications—make your business a marketing and fulfillment company. Your margins may be less, but you will not have to keep a plant running full-time. Additionally, running a manufacturing company requires very specific expertise. Investors and lenders will want to see a management team strong on production, distribution, and inventory management skills.

Many would-be entrepreneurs see opening a retail shop as their ultimate goal. But retailing is not for everyone. In the modern era, retailing is more than finding a good location on a busy street, near transportation, or within a pedestrian area; it is a sophisticated balance of inventory, product selection, and pricing. Retailing is not for the timid. Consider some of the issues:

▸ Stores frequently are open six or seven days a week (unless limited by local custom or laws), often eight to ten hours a day. This means that the store needs not only staff to greet and help customers but also an on-site manager.

▸ Retail employees, unless you are operating a high-end boutique, are poorly paid and tend to be temporary. It is hard to find and keep good retail workers.

▸ If you attempt (and you should) to keep wages and salaries in control, that means that you are running the store with few workers; if an employee is sick, needs time off, or quits, management (often you) has to fill in.

▸ Retail can require a good deal of initial cash in the start-up phase—not only initial inventory but also lease improvements, signs, fixtures, local licenses and permits, deposits, insurance, and other out-of-pocket expenses. The costs rise rapidly.

▸ Good locations are hard to find, and very good locations are expensive.

▸ Landlords are not going to rent a store to just anyone; they want to see that you have the ability to pay. Plan

on signing a long-term lease (at least several years)
and anticipate annual increases in rent.

▸ Utilities are costly. Witness the dramatic spike in
energy costs of the past several years. Good retail
ambience is expensive: signs, displays, coolers,
freezers, heating, and air conditioners. You have to
turn over a lot of inventory to just cover the basic
fixed costs.

▸ Owning a retail store, much like a restaurant, is a
lifestyle changer. If you have a spouse or partner,
you now have two. Even when the store is closed,
you have bills to pay, inventory to order, accounts
to balance, payroll to prepare (or better yet, have it
prepared), customer complaints, marketing, and a half
dozen other items that come up each week.

▸ Unlike other businesses, the value of a retail business
rarely goes up. Most retail operators do not own
the real estate in which the store is located. If you
sell a business that is successful (by comparable
standards) after ten years, you will get little in return.
The valuation will be based on the willingness of
some other person to take over the store—with a
minimal down payment. You will get the cost of your
inventory, a reduced valued for depreciated fixtures,
and some money for the goodwill and customer base
you have built up.

▸ Overall, the risk in retailing is high; no matter how
clever your concept, there are well-financed chains
and franchises that will be formidable competitors—
for the best locations, with efficient and professionally
managed operations, and with strong marketing.

If It Sounds Too Good to Be True, It Is

As you go through the process of searching for the right business idea, naturally you will jump to the Internet—that vast ocean of information, opinion, and near-fact. There are hundreds of reputable websites that offer both general and some very specific information that may be useful as you plan your business concept. In a week's time, you can get on enough e-mail lists to fill your in-box. Approach every source, every web page with great skepticism. In many ways, there is very little free high-quality information—the exception being the content that comes from government agencies, professional associations, and member groups.

Be particularly careful about blogs as a resource for specific information or industry data. Blogs are great fun and usually have a competent individual leading the way; they also attract people who seem to have nothing better to do than to make frivolous, fact-free comments. Nevertheless, the discriminating reader can glean some clever ideas and good ways to solve problems. Asking others who have been in the same situation can bring bounties of good, creative responses. Once again, you must ask yourself what to believe and what not to believe. A business or marketing blog run by a university professor is probably more reliable than a so-called business specialist with only general credentials. Look at the source before you spend valuable time.

Verify supposed "facts" before you use them—either in your business plan or as a basis for a business judgment—with some reliable source. Be very wary of offers that promise great earnings with little effort. These days a variety of cable and radio commercials offer a business concept tied to the Internet; you do not even have to take possession of the inventory. Products just sell themselves, and you end up with a glorious lifestyle—a big house, fancy car, and a boat to go with it all. You find these offers on the Internet as well—some not as obvious. Buy a book, CD, or training course (often rather expensive) or attend a free seminar run by professional salespeople, and you too can sell repossessed real estate, sell on eBay, or emulate a dozen other cookie-cutter concepts.

Count on this: the only person who makes money, despite the testimonials, is the publisher or promoter of the scheme. This kind of promotion is targeted at the weekend entrepreneur—not someone who is seriously thinking of making a financial and lifestyle change. Don't be fooled and don't be distracted. These appeals are compelling, especially if you are discouraged, concerned about losing your job, or under financial pressure; it sounds like for a few hundred dollars and minutes a day you can get started in a business and supplement your income. Don't be naive: making money is hard work (unless you are a trust-fund baby).

You should also apply caution when considering a myriad of business seminars that are highly touted. Many feature big-name sports legends and hugely successful businesspeople. Unlike a small-business fair or conference, these programs are designed to sell you a product or system. They are long on motivation and short on business technique and skills development. They can be interesting and entertaining—and they are also highly lucrative for their sponsors. Like everything else, you get what you pay for—in this case atmosphere and enthusiasm.

The Library: Free Information

It should be no surprise that your local library has a wealth of useful free information. One of the largest group of library patrons is businesspeople of all stripes. What the library offers is almost unlimited outreach and information. This information source is not just the stacks of books or racks of magazines in the physical space. The library also has sophisticated and talented reference specialists, who can help you find the information you need or find it for you. Almost every library is part of a cooperative lending consortium: if the material you want is not there, it can be borrowed from another institution.

But look beyond books to the countless databases and websites the library may subscribe to. You get unlimited search on some of the most prestigious business and professional sources available from some of the world's largest publishers. Your research potential for business ideas, help with your business plan, or new product development is limitless. Throughout this book you can find resources for specific books, databases, and websites that are helpful for the business owner.

It is important to distinguish what is available from what librarians know off the top of their heads. Be reasonable and do not expect reference librarians to know your facts for you. They are a resource and a guide, but you must know what you need and learn how to do the research yourself.

When doing your research, especially when using Google or other major search engines, it is easy to get lost in the maze of countless URLs. Furthermore, you can end up at sites that appear to be information-rich but in fact are created to sell you a product or service. The teaser copy is significant enough to attract your attention but not useful in its own right; to gain access to the meat of the site, you must pay a fee or purchase a product. As a general rule, don't bite. This same kind of content can be found on countless other websites or in books and other reference material—if you become an educated searcher.

Resources

USA Today

USA Today has a franchise locator that asks the amount of money you have in capital and what industry you are interested in, then provides a listing of franchises that match the two criteria: http://usatoday.franchisesolutions.com/top_franchises_info.cfm.

Franchise Business Review

Franchise Business Review (FBR) has recommendations on the best franchises to own. FBR is a national market research firm that conducts its own surveys to find out the level of franchisee satisfaction. It is particularly interested in areas such as training, support, operations, and the financial opportunity potentially enjoyed by the franchisee. This company lists the top fifty franchises for the year by three categories: large systems, midsize systems, and franchises with less than fifty units. The basic financial information is provided as well as hot links to more specialized content. Visit http://topfranchises.franchisebusinessreview.com to view these lists.

THREE

The Business Plan

Things to know before starting a business:

▶ *A business plan is your road map, even if a simple one.*

▶ *Writing a business plan can be an eye-opening experience.*

▶ *A business plan that emphasizes why your ideas are better is the goal of this exercise.*

▶ *Your financial projections must be realistic but still enticing to potential financiers.*

An Eye-Opening Experience

Simply stated, a business plan of whatever stripe is a road map to planning, organizing, financing, and operating a business. The degree of complexity (read size) of the business directly determines the degree of detail of the plan. Another way of stating this relationship is that the amount of money invested (or sought from investors or the bank) is directly proportional to the degree of detail in a plan.

A business plan is like a simulation or game: It allows you to try out your ideas without spending a fortune. It forces you to confront your own beliefs concerning the validity of your business concept. Take the simple (or not so simple) matter of financing the business. You envision a string of small boutique restaurants around the city center—your goal is to have five of them in operation over the next six years. Though this is an ambitious plan, you are convinced that you have a going concept and the ability to pull it off.

In the process of writing your business plan, you anticipate needing $500,000 per location, and you expect to pay for the second location from the cash flow of the first, and so on. You work carefully and diligently to the point where you know how many customers per day you need and what the average tab per customer must be in order to break even, make a modest profit, and generate sufficient revenue to build the $500,000 needed for the next location.

When this analysis is completed, you realize that you would have to be fully stocked with customers seven days a week, with an average food and beverage bill being over $45.00 per customer. It is immediately apparent that you cannot expect a restaurant to run full tilt all the time, generating maximum dollars. So now it is time to modify your original plan and, more important, your expectations about what is really possible. By taking the time to do the analysis, you have saved yourself a good deal of time, effort, and possibly money. You now know that you have to change your business concept and start over with different expectations.

Elements of a Business Plan

Every plan, no matter how detailed or how simplified, has common elements. Investors, bankers, vendors, and potential partners expect to find these in any business plan:

- summary of the plan—quick and dirty statement of overall goals
- description of the business you plan to start or buy
- statement of why your business will be unique—your market advantage
- overview of the current business environment—those items that will both help and hurt your business
- analysis of the competition—local, national, and even international depending on the kind and scope of business planned
- schedule for starting the business, including what is needed in terms of space, inventory, employees, software, and equipment
- three- to five-year financial plan—generally conservative, but with enough potential to be attractive to your audience
- detailed sales and marketing plan
- end/exit strategy—sell the business, merge with another, close down, and cash out and pay out

Summary of the Plan

The summary, or executive summary, is one of the smallest sections of your business plan. Even if your plan is simple, you should include a summary—if only a page or a few paragraphs. Readers want to get to the heart of the matter. If you are writing the plan to raise money, you should make a statement of financial need at the end of the summary.

In some cases, the summary could be an introductory paragraph and a series of bullet points each covering the elements of the business plan listed above. All sections of the plan should be summarized in the same order as the body of the business plan, using the same language. A summary is written after the rest of the business plan is finished, so you are sure that it is accurate and in the right order.

This is the hardest section to write because it must be brief but also interesting and entertaining. Yes, entertaining. You must grab the readers' attention with a strong opening statement:

> Smith Consulting will be successful because it is the only . . .
> No other restaurant will have . . .
> There is no product on the market that competes with . . .
> The better mousetrap has been developed, and it is called . . .

Description of the Business

Leave nothing to the imagination; assume readers know absolutely nothing about business, and especially about your planned business. Give them the details in short, simple descriptive paragraphs with subheads to show logic and order in your narration.

Start with an overview that provides the key elements of your business: what you do, who does it, why it is needed, and how you will compete effectively. Every business needs a mission statement (what your company will do), goals (critical milestones that will indicate success and profitability), values (principles that guide your actions), and vision (to be the best, largest, fastest growing).

Describing your products or services can be tricky; make it simple and nontechnical. The readers at this stage do not need to know or understand the intricacies of your product line. But do take the time to explain why it is needed, what is unique about the services, what problems you solve for the customer, who needs your products, and why they need them. Though you will discuss the market and business environment in more detail later, in this section do spend a bit of time linking your products or services to the current environment and explain your critical advantage. Think in terms of cheaper, faster, better, more features, underserved market, solving problems, and so forth.

No business plan ignores negatives: problems, concerns, entrenched competition, costs, distribution difficulties, key personnel needed, the bad economic environment—whatever is present and of concern. You always need to discuss pros and cons; to avoid problems and concentrate only on the positive is both unrealistic and unbusinesslike. Readers know that nothing runs smoothly or easily. Show your business maturity and acumen by anticipating and facing the business and financial reality before you. Some experts refer to this as SWOT analysis: *strengths, weaknesses, opportunities*, and *threats*.

It is important to demonstrate clearly and firmly why you (and your team—partners or key employees) have the experience and skill to run this business successfully. This is not the time to be shy or assume readers know you and your abilities. Tell them what you have done in the past, and link these skills and experience directly to your new venture. Do the same for partners and key employees—make sure every functional area of the business is covered—finance, marketing, operations, technology, and distribution.

Add a short checklist on special issues that will affect your company now and in the longer term. Answer these questions simply or indicate that they are discussed later in the plan:

Are your products prone to obsolescence (technology)?

Is your business seasonal (garden center)?

How important is your location? (If a retail store, this is very important.)

How much customer contact? (Web businesses may have very little.)

Are there special skills needed, such as design or research?

Is your industry a mature or a fast-growing one?

These are but a small sample of the kinds of issues that may require special treatment. Ask your advisors or business coach to help you identify any that are specific to your business concept. It is always best to confront problems and demonstrate clearly that you are on top of the situation.

At some point, explain how your company will be legally structured: as a corporation, partnership, sole proprietorship, or limited liability company. This is a good time to discuss current ownership (if there are silent partners or investors) and, if seeking financial backing from investors (as opposed to a loan from the bank), how much of the company equity is available as a percentage to new investors.

Finally, mention any patents, trademarks, and copyrights owned by the company as well as awards, recognition within the industry, and other significant intangible assets the company owns.

Statement of Why Your Business Will Be Unique

Unique is one of the most abused words in the English language. It cannot be modified. There is no such thing as "more unique" or "highly unique." Unique is just unique; the word stands alone. Though it may be difficult to claim uniqueness, you must accept the challenge of telling your audience why your business concept is fundamentally better than what is out there; why you will succeed when others have failed; and how you can, by product mix or level of service, gain market traction quickly. Not easy, is it?

The way to approach this is to separate all the elements of your business, your product, and your service level and indicate how each is superior to your competition's. Here are but a few of the issues you might present in your attempt to convince readers that you have something, well, unique:

Is the technology better, simpler, faster?

How about packaging and product presentation?

Can you command attention because of your quality?

What about pricing?

Can you be first or second to the market with new products?

Is your service better or cheaper?

Is your product user-friendly?

Does your product have a long shelf life?

How about flexible manufacturing?

Is your brand strong and growing?

Do you have a niche service business?

Is there little price sensitivity? (How nice if true.)

To answer these kinds of questions, you are really going to have to dig. Obviously, if you can find one or two very strong points that speak to your business, that is all that is required. But your proof and support need to be convincing. Just because you say it is so does not demonstrate a market or product advantage. Use charts, graphs, pictures, and data to demonstrate. Be specific and compare apples to apples with the competition. Know your costs, prices, features, market penetration, demographics, and other details.

Traditional sources such as the reference desk at the library are a huge help, but the Internet can potentially answer just about any question or provide data on any topic you need for your business plan. As discussed in chapter 2, the problem you face is determining the accuracy of the data. The various free encyclopedias are excellent for basic content and generally are accurate. The best sources of information are government websites, industry groups, the competitors' sites, and sites for which a fee is paid to join. No matter the origin of your facts and figures, cite your sources.

Overview of the Current Business Environment

You cannot control the overall business climate, but you can tell your audience how you plan to function within it, especially if times are tough. It is always more difficult to raise money or establish credit in a recession or a time of slowing economic growth. Lenders, vendors, and investors alike become more conservative, and rates tend to go up, reflecting the general concern about economic growth. The basic premise is simple: If unemployment is higher and economic growth is stagnant, businesses and consumers both tighten their belts and spend less. On the other hand, when times are good and growth is strong, there is always plenty of money available. It may not be in the form you prefer (equity as opposed to bank loan), but it is there.

Speak directly about how you will manage in the current and near-term economic environment. Explain how you will start or build your business without excessive risk. Be specific. In hard times, you might plan and propose the following:

Buy used office furniture and equipment.
Lease rather than buy.
Start the business from home rather than rent space.

Start part-time, while keeping your full-time job.

Take a small salary or none at all.

Employ part-time workers with limited benefits.

Use contract workers rather than hire employees.

Outsource expensive services, such as accounting or
website development.

Offer bare-bones benefits.

Have slow plans for growth until conditions improve.

No single entrepreneur can manage everything; you will need help. Demonstrate that you are open to advice and counsel by forming an advisory board (or more formally a board of directors, if you are large enough). Make sure that your accountant or other financial expert is part of that board. Even if your advisors are limited to the banker and your business coach, you at least demonstrate your flexibility and your concern about getting and following solid business advice.

Always have a contingency plan. Don't just describe your "Plan B"; make it concrete with numbers.

	Plan A	Plan B
Start-up capital:	$300,000	$200,000
Revenue:	$700,000	$500,000
Salaries:	$150,000	$ 80,000
Overhead:	$100,000	$ 70,000
Cost of goods sold:	$ 80,000	$ 60,000
Marketing/sales:	$100,000	$ 85,000

One caution: be careful what you propose to cut in Plan B. Reductions in salaries and overhead show prudent management and a frugal cost basis. Cutting marketing too much may affect your ability to reach your revenue goals, making the whole plan look weak.

Analysis of the Competition

If you are new to a business, this part of the plan is much more difficult—hence the reason entrepreneurs should not stray too far from what they know. Nevertheless, experienced or not, the information is all there; you just have to find it and organize it so that it is clear and concise.

If your business is regional, and most new businesses are, focus on the local competition. If you are starting a new marketing consultancy firm, for example, the huge national (or international) firms are not necessarily your competitors. Your former employer and two or three regional firms may be. Your competitors can be both direct and indirect. The former do exactly what you plan to do; the latter offer similar services, but not exactly like yours. This group is competition because their general services might easily be expanded to include what you plan to offer.

It is essential to get specific. Build a spreadsheet, something like that shown in exhibit 3-1, that provides as much detail as possible about the competition.

There is an old saying: keep your friends close and your enemies (competition) even closer. Get to know your competitors. Visit their place of business if you can; talk to former employees, colleagues in the industry, vendors, and even lenders. People may be bound by contract and commitment to be discreet, but with each contact you can get some information that will help you build a competitor profile.

One way to learn about your competitors is to buy from them. You can examine their products and services, pricing, and customer

EXHIBIT 3-1 ▸ **Competitor Profiles**

	Competitor A	Competitor B	Competitor C
Name			
Public/Private			
Direct/Indirect			
Size			
Sales per Employee			
Services/ Products			
Market			
Distribution			
Market Share			
Pricing			
Key Benefits of Products			
Managerial Strengths			
Service			
Technology			
Website			

service and generally get a sense of where they have been and where they are going. Pay particular attention to new product announcements, joint ventures, or new marketing programs. You should have in your possession every piece of literature: sales catalogs, brochures, press releases, financial statements (if possible), and any other public document you can get your hands on (without doing anything unethical or illegal to gain access to information). Most of all, study and know the details of competitors' websites. What do they have that you need; why is yours better? Finally, sign up for your competitor's online newsletter or e-mail blasts. You will learn a lot quickly.

Not everyone is your competitor; this identification process can get out of hand, confusing rather than educating readers. Too much information, especially in a short business plan, is worse that too little. Identify two or three competitors and offer as much detail as you can within a few pages. You may not have to leave your computer workstation to get much of this information. Google deep into the name—you will be amazed at what can show up.

Above all else, be positive. Don't trash the competition—in print or when competing for customers. Tell why you are better, faster, cheaper—whatever benefits you have identified.

Schedule for Starting the Business

If you are buying an existing business, then your "start of business" is when you take over the company. If you are beginning from scratch, you want to identify specifically when you will launch and why that is a good time to do so. If you have a seasonal retail business, it is normally a bad idea to open once the season has begun. You have to be ready and fully stocked and staffed a month or two beforehand.

Here is the ideal place to make your business concrete. Give the details as to employees needed at start-up, in six months, and, say, in two years. Don't just list employees, inventory, computers, office equipment, space needs, and other equipment; also give some realistic costs for these start-up items. These same numbers will be incorporated into your financial forecast in the next section.

Three- to Five-Year Financial Plan

This may be the most important part of the business plan, and for those with limited financial background difficult to put together. This is essentially a forecast, based on the company's past financial experiences (if there are any) or the financial goals or milestones your new company wishes to achieve over the near term.

If the company exists and has a history, a five-year plan is better than a three-year plan. If the company is brand new, go only three years. (In either case, five-year projections are just plain guesses. No one can know what will happen in five years.) In all cases, especially if you are trying to attract lenders or experienced investors, keep you numbers somewhat conservative but interesting enough to attract their attention. This is a tricky line to walk.

In effect, you are telling everyone who reads this plan what your capital requirements are going to be to start this business; this is your *capital investment*—money spent before you even open your doors. In addition, you are also going to detail your initial *working capital* needs—the capital requirement needed to operate the business.

Almost everyone underestimates the cash requirements—both capital investment and working capital. Every entrepreneur feels that they can build a business on a shoestring, that the customers will come rolling in and the business will be cash-flow positive much sooner than is realistically the case. If you need $100,000, try to get $150,000—just in case. Remember (from chapter 1) that more businesses go out of business because of liquidity problems than for any other reason.

Recall that a product business costs more to start and operate than a service business, as the following comparison shows:

	Capital Spending: Product Business	Capital Spending: Service Business
Computers, furniture	Needed	Needed
Office supplies	Needed	Needed
Telephone and computers	Needed	Needed
Utility deposits/payments	Needed	Needed
Marketing materials/web page	Needed	Needed
Build-out for store or plant	Needed	May not have any expenses, for example, by working at home
Office space	Needed	May or may not be needed
Shelving, displays	Needed	None or minimal
Manufacturing costs	Needed	None
Inventory costs	Needed	None
Warehousing	Needed	None

To make this all work and appear unified and cohesive, you need to build cash flow statements for each of the years outlined in your plan (in most cases three statements are needed). You can build this on a monthly or quarterly basis; the latter is easier and allows for unexpected changes in one month that could be made up in the third month of the quarter. Besides, it is extremely difficult and tedious to estimate exactly what you will spend each month and what income will come in each month. A simple spreadsheet template allows you to make changes, with only basic spreadsheet skills needed.

Cash flow statements report a company's inflow and outflow of cash. Monitoring cash flow is important because a company needs enough cash on hand to pay its expenses and purchase assets. An income statement can tell you whether a company made a profit; a cash flow statement can tell you whether the company will stay in business. A cash flow statement shows changes over time rather than absolute dollar amounts at a point in time. It uses and reorders the information from a company's balance sheet and income statement. See chapter 8, Finance Basics, for details on the structure of cash flow statements.

Sales and Marketing Plan

How you are going to market and sell your products and services is as critical as any information contained in the business plan. It is one thing to say that you will open a boutique in a high-income suburb; it is another entirely to present your store and your merchandise to the right market, with the right mix, and at the right price. Among the many tasks is to identify your customer:

- Realistically, who will buy your or similar products or services. Be specific.
- Profile the customer by age, income level, job description, location; it is worthwhile to include demographic statistics to support your claims.
- What is the size of your potential audience?
- How and where do they make their purchases: Internet, mass-market store, boutique, catalog?
- Do you sell luxury goods or necessities?
- Is your business seasonal?
- Who makes the decisions about buying, and how long does it take?
- Are your customers potentially repeat customers?

There are many different answers, depending on whether you are a consumer marketer or a business-to-business marketer; whether you sell through a retail business or just on the Internet; or whether you sell a product or a service. In the best of all worlds, you will be in a business where there is demand for your products, potential for repeat customers (the products are consumable or become obsolescent), year-round sales to a specific market that is accessible via standard marketing tools, and a customer base sufficiently large to actually earn you a profit. It is just that easy!

Some of the research completed on the competition will overlap and help with your marketing plan. You may need to conduct direct marketing research (as opposed to indirect research from secondary sources, such as government reports) through direct surveys or other vehicles with potential customers. You could call existing customers on the phone, prepare an online survey that you ask people to fill out, stand in the parking lot of a shopping mall and ask buyers questions, or send out a survey via e-mail. Your goal is to quantify the results, so the questions must be simple with easy choices: yes, no, true, false, ask for a number, price, which of three models, and so forth.

At some point you must explain how you will get your customers' attention: this is not easy, but there are dozens of specific campaigns you can put into place. Consider some of the following:

- Buzz marketing: good old-fashioned word-of-mouth, where one person tells another—movies and songs are sold this way all the time.
- Social networking through Google+, Facebook, Twitter, and LinkedIn, for example, are all the rage.
- Search engine optimization (SEO) works to get your company higher in Internet search profiles.
- Free webinars—but they have to be more than advertisement for your company.

- A free app that ties in to your company or services.
- Networking: who do you know who can introduce you to other people? Think about your current clients, friends, coworkers, and even vendors.
- Business cards.
- Interviews, writing a column in a newsletter, and press releases are among a few media events that can be used effectively.
- E-mail blasts, although it takes time to build a database of prospects and customers.
- Direct mail: Large postcards are used frequently. They are cheap and get attention. Catalogs and brochures are expensive, but they can work.
- Stuffers and promo items: put new product announcements into invoices, statements, and other general correspondence.
- Signs, banners, balloons, billboards, and benches are all good ways to announce your business.

Marketing campaigns do not have to be expensive, but you need to market regularly and often. You will have to give the campaigns time to work; not every response is immediate. Most of all, indicate in your business plan how you will track your efforts to find out which works best for your particular business. As important, do not overspend; pace your marketing and your marketing costs until you know what works and what does not.

Exit Strategy

If you are writing a business plan specifically for investors, this is an important issue. At some point, investors will want their principal back—whether loans or stock, they will want to cash out. Some companies are built with a specific time line, such as in five years the business will be sold or investors will be replaced with other kinds of financing.

Though no one wants to admit the possibility that the business might fail, this is also a good time to remind investors—yet again—that there is risk involved. Recognize this possibility, but don't dwell on it.

If your plan is not being written for investors, this section is less important. Nevertheless, lenders and vendors want to know what your ultimate goal is—sell the company, merge with other groups, pass it on to the children, or some other vision.

Resources

Small Business Administration

The Small Business Administration has an excellent site that includes resources for writing a business plan. Visit www.sba.gov and click on the tab "Starting and Managing a Business."

Business Plans Kit for Dummies

Business Plans Kit for Dummies (For Dummies, 2010) has all the forms referred to in the book electronically stored on the accompanying CD, in both MS Word and PDF formats. An e-book version of basically the same content is available at a cheaper price, but it does not include the forms.

The Ernst & Young Business Plan Guide

Now in its third edition, *The Ernst & Young Business Plan Guide* (Wiley, 2007) is a classic book from one of the largest accounting and consulting companies in the world. The "dos" and "don'ts" are very helpful, as is the sample business plan. It is, however, focused on products as opposed to services, which is a bit of a drawback.

Writing a Convincing Business Plan

Also in its third edition, *Writing a Convincing Business Plan* (Barron's Educational Series, 2008) is best used by those who know the basics of writing a business plan. If your plan is simple, this may be more detailed than you will need or want. Nevertheless, it's one of the overall better plan books available.

Encyclopedia of Business

A free online version of the *Encyclopedia of Business* can be found at www.referenceforbusiness.com/small. Articles are organized alphabetically; simply click on the term, and an extended article is available. Although the references in the articles are dated, basic descriptions of business terms and related concepts are timeless.

FOUR

Taking Stock of Your Finances

Things to know before starting a business:

- ▸ *Personal solvency is critical to starting a business.*
- ▸ *Lenders and investors will be evaluating your financial acumen.*
- ▸ *A bank loan is good, but equity is better.*
- ▸ *There are many ways to finance a business, but some affect you personally more than others.*

Personal Finance and Business Finance

Living in a financial dream world and starting a business are just not compatible. There is absolutely no reason not to understand both the status of your personal finances and the basics of financial management of a business (see chapter 8 for a financial primer).

There are literally thousands of websites, courses, books, magazines, and seminars available to you to supplement what follows in this chapter.

In some ways finance is finance, whether personal or business. Cash is and always will be king. If you do not have enough of it, if it is not earned or paid to you on time and regularly, you cannot meet your obligations. It is as simple as that. The trick is both knowing what sufficient capital is and having the discipline to put together a plan to ensure that you have the cash necessary both to sustain your current living standard and build your business.

A Personal Financial Analysis

The first task is taking stock of your personal resources—meaning cash on hand, investments, retirement funds, insurance, educational funds, real estate, and other real or disposable property. This, of course, also means balancing these assets against your liabilities: your mortgage payment, living expenses, credit card and auto payments, utilities, and educational expenses. Remember to include seasonal and emergency expenses, such as holiday gifts, travel, and house repairs. A simple personal balance sheet like the one shown in exhibit 4-1 will help you understand your current financial position.

It is easy to fool yourself into believing that your furniture, eight-year-old boat, or the two cars in the driveway are worth much more than they are should you actually try to sell them. It is also easy to overstate the value of your home or other real estate. Because there is a glut of property for sale these days, and as prices have gone down (especially sharply in some overbuilt regions), you must use values that reflect the current reality, or this exercise

EXHIBIT 4-1 ▶ **Assets and Liabilities: Annual Survey**

Assets		Liabilities		Net Difference
House	$_____	Total house expense	$(_____)	$_____
Car	$_____	Balance of car loan	$(_____)	$_____
Personal goods	$_____	Installment loans/credit cards	$(_____)	$_____
Stocks and bonds	$_____	Health, life, and property insurance	$(_____)	$_____
Annuities and insurance	$_____	Taxes due on sale/from income	$(_____)	$_____
Savings account	$_____	Bank loans/student loans	$(_____)	$_____
Investment property	$_____	Mortgage loan	$(_____)	$_____
Rental income	$_____	Maintenance and taxes	$(_____)	$_____
Other assets	$_____	Other expenses	$(_____)	$_____
Total	$_____	Total	$(_____)	$_____

is of little help. There are a variety of sources for solid information for valuing both real estate and automobiles, and any other real property. Your local real estate agent can help, as can online websites like Zillow (www.zillow.com). And, of course, the stock and bond markets give you immediate feedback about what your market investments are worth.

Your personal income statement is a snapshot of what you earn on a monthly basis, including any money from investments, retirement schemes, alimony/child support, and any other legal income. Against these are all the day-to-day expenses you pay out during the month. This exercise can be extremely revealing—especially if you are brutally honest about what you really spend (and on what) as opposed to what you think you spend.

Financial planners to a person will ask you to spend one month carefully recording every expenditure you make, no matter how small; the result could look something like exhibit 4-2. This includes buying a newspaper or magazine and spending on food, clothing, and entertainment. You must record all the incidentals: lunch at work, coffee on the way to work, movie rentals, and so on, including all your transportation costs. If you have a spouse, both parties have to be equally honest if you are going to get a true picture of your income and expenses.

Managing Money

The scary part of really looking at your monthly income and expenses, as most people understand intuitively, is that there is not much left after everything has been paid. Remember, this is cash in and cash out, so even savings and retirement money are still cash out. Both are obviously good practices, as is any investment plan

EXHIBIT 4-2 ▸ **Monthly Income and Expenses**

Income

Wages/salary	$5,000
Annuities	$ 0
Retirement income	$ 0
Child support	$1,000
Investment income	$ 280
Interest	$ 20
Part-time work wages	$ 0
Rental income	$ 0
Other	$ 0
Total Income	$6,300

Expenses

Mortgage/rent	$1,350
Home repairs	$ 75
Food	$ 600
Clothing	$ 200
Transportation	$ 175
Auto payment	$ 300
Auto repair	$ 0
Entertainment	$ 125
All taxes	$ 800
Tuition	$ 0
Loans	$ 0
Charge cards	$ 225
All insurance	$ 600
Child care	$ 700
Utilities	$ 350
Savings and investments	$ 500
Total Expenses	$6,000
Net Cash after Expenses	$ 300

you have in place. If you are like most people, and you want to start a business, your cash position is probably fair to weak.

You have to go on a money diet; the best advice is to look carefully at what you spend and make some hard decisions. Your ultimate goal is to increase savings and other investments to build up your personal balance sheet sufficiently to both start the business and sustain you for the first months or even a year or two. After that, if things go well, you can get other financing to run the business, including income from the business itself.

One of the classic financial planner tricks is to ask a client to skip the morning coffee stop and replace it with coffee from home or a less expensive fast food outlet. Some people who enjoy several cups of gourmet coffee a day find that they can save hundreds in a month's time. This is a simple but clear example of the kind of behavior change you may have to undertake to build up your nest egg and have money for your business.

The ultimate goal of all of this is to increase your assets and reduce your debts. For many people, credit cards have the highest interest rates. Suppose you have five credit cards, all with some balance. Take the lowest balance (assuming most of the finance charges are about the same interest rate) and work it off aggressively. Never pay just minimums. Once you have picked off one card, attack the next lowest, and so on.

This tactic assumes that you have the discipline to change your life from a credit card junkie to a cash-paying customer. Use your debit card instead of a credit card—you will soon know when you have run out of money. Keep one or two credit cards open for emergencies—when using them is absolutely justified. But an emergency is not a big sale at the boutique or a new set of golf clubs.

If you are married or have children, everyone in the family has to be a partner in the new savings behavior. You cannot have one spouse making sacrifices and the other spending as before. Having full family support is so important. If everyone is not on board, there will be problems, tension, and hard feelings. You need not live like monks, but if you are generally honest and sincere about having a business at some point, you have to get your personal spending and your credit history in line.

Personal Credit and Financing Your Business ·····

Let's imagine that through hard work and diligence you have saved sufficient money to begin your new business (even part-time) and pay for everyday living expenses for at least six months, with a bit more on the side for emergencies. This alone is an impressive feat.

At some point in a business start-up phase, most entrepreneurs will be on the hunt for additional capital, beyond their personal resources, to grow the business. Typically one might look to family members, take on a partner with deeper pockets, or take out a business loan through a bank or government-sponsored entity designed to foster new business development. Your ability to find additional capital for a growing business, especially in the first year or two, is directly related to the quality of your own personal credit history. The notion is quite simple: if you have had the maturity and good sense to manage your personal finances, it seems reasonable that you can then manage the business's finances and thus are creditworthy.

It is standard operating procedure for all credit grantors (banks, charge cards, store credit cards, auto loan companies) to look at your credit report and your credit score (FICO). The credit score is a numerical expression of an individual's creditworthiness. It is an estimate of an individual's ability to repay debt and to do it on time. Scores are based on information obtained by credit bureaus or credit reference agencies. The higher the score, the more likely you are to obtain credit. Scores are based on such factors as payment history (good or bad, judgments, and missed or late payments), amount owed, length of credit history (stability), new credit, and the types of credit used (charge card versus mortgages).

When you are starting out with your business, most banks or vendors ask you to be personally responsible for a business loan or line of credit. Simply, if the business cannot pay, the owners must. All lenders want as much collateral (as an incentive to repay) as possible on a business loan. When it comes time to get your first real business loan, expect the banker to want to secure the loan with all of the business's cash, investments, receivables, inventory, and possibly other assets—plus your personal guarantee. If the loan request is large enough, the banker may ask for other security, such as rental property or your home. I strongly recommend that you never put up your place of residence as collateral for a business loan. This puts you (and your family) in great peril. You never quite know what is going to happen. Always anticipate that your business will be a roaring success, but know that businesses do fail.

In the early stages of a business, you personally *are* your business—especially when it comes to guarantees on business loans. Your personal finances, again, are a reflection of what the bank can expect in terms of your business financial sophistication and your ability to manage money. Nevertheless, it is always best not to mingle business finance and personal finance. Even the tiniest of home businesses should have separate checking accounts for personal money and cash from your business. The same is true with loans and credit cards. You may have to back the first line of credit with the bank personally, and you may have to use your personal credit card for travel and other expenses, but as soon as possible, work with your banker to get off the hook for business loans. Further, get a credit card in the name of the company, not in yours, as soon as you can.

There are other reasons not to commingle personal and business funds; doing so can cause problems at tax time. If you get audited (and even if you don't), it is going to be extremely difficult to track business income and expenses. Furthermore, it looks unprofessional: Paying an important vendor with a personal check makes you look small-time. Have and use company checks; it shows outsiders that you have a going concern. When you commingle personal with business funds, it is easy to make mistakes and much more difficult to have a clear audit trail as well. Finally, this practice may make it more difficult to judge how the business really did.

Similarly, do your best not to guarantee vendor agreements. Do not be surprised that your first orders with some vendors must be paid up front (or at least with a substantial down payment) before the order is processed. The more you do business with vendors, the more willing they are to extend credit—to a point. Every customer, no matter how large, will have a credit limit. Your salespeople will do their best to get that extended, and the controllers of the companies will do their best to limit the vendor's exposure.

It is not uncommon for people with small businesses to use their personal credit cards to finance a business. This can be done. Many people can get multiple credit cards, and when the entire available credit line is added up, it can result in tens of thousands, and more. This is one approach to financing the business; it is also an expensive one and offers you absolutely no protection if the company fails. The debt is yours personally, not the company's. If you start out this way, that may be just fine, but as soon as possible, move the debt from your personal responsibility to the company.

Concerns about company debt should motivate you to ensure that you are incorporated; this way, the company's business (especially its debts and any lawsuits) is legally separated from you personally. This is just another example of keeping business and personal assets differentiated. The most popular is some form of limited liability company; the structure of such companies is similar but not the same in the United States and Canada. Shareholders in limited liability companies are not responsible for company debts, although directors may be required to guarantee loans or credit granted to the company. There are details about incorporation in chapter 5.

Banker's Perspective

Some small-business owners do not see themselves or their businesses as candidates for a bank loan or line of credit. They may be right if both their personal and business financial histories are checkered. Funding for your new venture is crucial, so this is not the time to be timid. Unless you plan to keep the business very small and informal, you will need capital other than your own at some point.

Sit in a banker's chair for a moment and look at the world from that perspective. First and foremost, bankers and banks are motivated to find and build a portfolio of loan customers—especially companies that are growing. The whole nature of banking is built on customer relationships that generate fees for services and interest income from loans. Business bankers are hired not only to process paper but to seek new customers actively. They sell for a living.

The bank makes money by collecting funds—savings and checking accounts, money market accounts—and lending to businesses and consumers. Business lending and other finance services are very profitable for banks—assuming the loans are of good quality.

Frequently, depositors leave vast sums in checking accounts that pay little or no interest; this money is then available to the bank to lend or invest; the spread between the interest it charges or earns and the interest it pays depositors is one of the prime sources of revenue. Banks also collect funds by charging origination and loan termination fees, collecting extra on late payments, charging for wire transfer services and letters of credit, and even charging for loans paid early.

Nevertheless, the banking community can be very conservative. *Risk* is a nasty word and one that is to be avoided at all costs. Bankers see hundreds of loan applications in any one month and probably choose to write very few loans based on these applications. Some customers are simply naive about the process, the purpose of the loan, the amount of the loan, the importance of a relationship, good credit, and a host of other issues. A bank loan can be even harder to get if the current economic environment is poor. Periodically bankers become even more risk adverse and lend only to the best customers; they, like everyone else, are concerned about liquidity and cash flow when times are tough.

Remember, too, that not all banks are the same. Community banks are focused on the local clients. They tend to be generalists and are probably better at handling the basics such as checking, savings, and car and home loans. But many have a small-business banking section, specifically to handle the needs of their retail customers and other small businesses in the area. They have much smaller lending limits by charter and do not have the sophisticated services that the mega-banks have. They also may be more approachable if you are part of their immediate market. The national banks have responded to the local community concept—close to the customer—by filling up almost any open storefront in city and suburban neighborhoods with small branch banks. They want the customers to come into the lobby of the bank, where they can offer everything from basic services to insurance and investments—and loans. The business loan department may be cities away, but you can get local service just the same.

The way to get a bank loan is to plan for it. Develop a relationship with the bank and a loan officer. Open a business checking account and be absolutely scrupulous that your minimum required balance is always in place. Move your personal checking to this bank, and if it is competitive, get your home and car loans there as well as an equity line of credit. Need a lock box? Other banking services? Do it all at the same place.

If possible, arrange a very small business loan—say a few thousand. Be timely in your payments, and in six months you can ask to have the line extended. In a year you will be in a position to ask for what you really need. One loan officer put the matter succinctly: the main requirements for attaining a small business loan are your personal credit history, business plan, experience, education, and feasibility of the business you are starting or expanding.

There is an old axiom in the loan business that obtaining a loan requires meeting the "Five Cs": character, collateral, conditions, capacity, and capital. Even in the impersonal world of banking, *character* still counts for something—thus the importance of the bank getting to know you. Make it clear that you do volunteer work, have children in the local school, or are active in other pursuits. Your credit history speaks volumes about your character. Personal stability is important. Few loans are ever given without some form of *collateral;* even so-called signature loans have your credit rating as the last backup for collection. *Conditions* are the purpose or use of the loan—thus the importance of a good business plan. Buying new equipment meets the condition criterion; buying a new car for the business owner may not be an appropriate use of the loan. *Capacity* is your ability to pay. If you do not have income or an obvious means to pay back the loan, your chances are slim or none. A banker likes to see that you have personally invested your own money in the business; the more *capital* you have invested, the greater your chances for a loan. If you are not willing to risk your own money in this new business venture, why would the bank?

As you develop and grow your business relationship with the banker, be willing to share information. See the banker as a partner, not an adversary. Even if the information is not always great, share it anyway. At least once a year, if you have a substantial outstanding balance, you will have to submit financial statements—so your banker is going to find out the good, the bad, and the ugly anyway. Help the banker understand your business. Each kind of business

---

Who Borrows?

The Small Business Association reported in 2008 that the percentage of small firms using credit varied directly with firm size. The percentage of firms using any credit increased from 70 percent to 99.6 percent as the employment size of the firms increased from 0 to over 100. This relationship was most evident in small firms' use of credit from loans supplied by depository institutions (banks, thrifts, etc.). For example, only 22 percent of firms with no employees used credit from depository institutions, whereas 78 percent of firms with more than 100 employees used depository institutions.

---

has unique wrinkles. One company, a technical book publisher, spent time educating its bank about accounts receivable for wholesalers and large booksellers. It was (and still is) customary to pay in 90 days rather than the usual 30 days. International sales often took

120 to 150 days to be paid. Once the banker understood this and saw this trend over time, she was much more comfortable about how the company was being operated.

Don't be afraid to ask business associates, friends, and relatives to make introductions: Getting a referral from an existing customer is how many banks build their loan portfolio. This referral process often reassures the banker that the potential customer is a known entity with ties to the local business community. Where do your vendors bank? Your lawyer, accountant, and business coach, because they are familiar with your business, may be able to direct you to the right bank for your business and help you build a solid banking relationship.

Guarantees

Nothing makes a banker happier than making a loan with little or no risk. One way to reduce the risk is have a cosigner or other guarantor for a loan. Cosigners are typically used when there is insufficient credit history or the credit history (personal or business) is not strong. Few people with resources and excellent credit histories are going to volunteer to put themselves in harm's way by agreeing to cosign a business loan. Your partner would have to; you spouse might be willing. There have even been cases when a vendor provided a guarantee in order to keep someone's business coming, though such vendors would not extend themselves without some kind of personal guarantee or equity stake in the business. In fact, ownership or an interest in the business can often be the best incentive for a friend or relative to participate in financing a business.

There are other kinds of guarantors: Government agencies, either national level or regional, have programs to promote small business development and expansion. Tax incremental financing districts (TIFs), regional development corporations, and even the federal government through the Small Business Administration have loan programs that guarantee payment to the bank in the event of default or business failure. (If you fail to pay, that does not mean that the loan goes away—you may just owe a different master.) You can go directly to these government entities, or you can work through a participating bank. In either case, they offer one of the best alternatives for financing through traditional lending institutions because they are set up to manage the risk involved with small-business creation and development.

One final word on bank financing: banks by charter have credit limits on what they can lend to whom. However, most banks can accommodate a loan request of $100,000 or less relatively simply. If your requirements are greater than this, anticipate a good deal more paperwork, a more sophisticated business plan, and a good deal more selling. Larger loan applications go before the loan committee at the bank, and many require an initial audit of your business. Quarterly income statements, balance sheets, and statements of cash flow plus an annual audit may be part of the loan covenants.

Alternative Financing

Banks are not the only lenders small-business owners may take advantage of—but you must understand them well so that they don't take unexpected advantage of you.

Leasing

One alternative to a bank loan or line of credit is leasing. The leasing industry is huge—for everything from personal automobiles to aircraft for major airlines. Almost any tangible business asset can be leased:

computers, servers, and peripherals

networks

software

forklifts

trucks and heavy equipment

conveyors

furniture

security systems

medical equipment

restaurant equipment

telecom systems

buildings

The list goes on and on.

Leasing may be easier than obtaining a loan because the financial requirements are not as strict. The equipment itself is the security for the lease. If you fail to pay, the leasing company takes the leased equipment. Simple as that. And there are further advantages. Leasing is considered off-balance-sheet financing, so it does not use up your capital or available lines of credit. Instead of spending tens of thousands to outfit an office, you instead have a manageable monthly payment.

Another big advantage is that leasing also allows you the opportunity to update your old equipment constantly. This means the immediate competitive edge of having the latest technology and the long-term benefit of not having to worry about your equipment becoming outdated. For instance, we all know how quickly computer technology improves, creating an obsolescence risk whenever new hardware and software are purchased. By using business equipment leasing as a financing tool, you can update that technology every few years, without having to worry about disposing of your out-of-date, depreciated equipment.

A final important benefit is that business equipment leasing allows you to get what you need now rather than wait for receivables and your cash flow to improve. Having to buy equipment a piece at a time could damage your business operations and give your competitors an edge. Why take that risk, when a business equipment lease can solve the problem? However, and this is important, leasing can be expensive. You need to compare the costs carefully. Do you really need the newest and best every three years? You are responsible for maintenance of leased equipment, and there are limits to its use—maybe 10,000 miles a year for a leased car. Going over that amount is costly.

Peer-to-Peer Lenders

In an environment of generally tightening credit, even leasing may not be an option; if standards get tight enough, and they can, another alternative is peer-to-peer lenders such as Prosper, Lending Club, and Zopa. These are online forums through which entrepreneurs looking for a cash fix can find unsecured loans from willing lenders. The amount available is typically $25,000 or less—so this source may be a small and temporary fix to a cash-flow need. The three peer-to-peer lenders mentioned above each work a bit differently. Prosper, for example, is a bid site like eBay: you post the amount you want to borrow and the interest rate you are willing to pay, and bidders make offers.

For business owners, the attraction to peer-to-peer lending is simple: They are often able to get loans more easily and cheaply than they would from a traditional lender. Start-ups have long found that their limited track record makes it difficult to secure lines of credit or conventional bank loans. But now, as a result of the credit crisis and softening economy, even established businesses are finding it difficult to find additional capital.

There is one important feature of these kinds of loans. They are not traditional business-to-business loans but rather personal loans that are being used for business purposes. If you borrow this way, your credit score may be affected, since this loan is no different than an additional charge card or a new auto loan. Zopa bases lending decisions on your personal credit history. In fact, when applying for a loan, you must provide your social security number so that a thorough credit check can be made.

Be Aware of Scams

Advance-fee loans (not to be confused with peer-to-peer loans) are usually, if not always, empty promises of a personal or business loan requiring payment of a fee in advance. Fraudulent advance-fee loan schemes generally prey on vulnerable consumers—the unemployed, those who have bad credit ratings, or small business owners in immediate need of money.

Ads promising "money to loan . . . regardless of credit history" lure consumers into paying fees that range from $25 to several hundred dollars, in advance of supposedly receiving loans that are guaranteed. Often these ads feature 1-900 numbers, which result in charges on your phone bill, or toll-free 1-800 numbers.

The fee may be referred to as "processing," "application," or "first month's payment." Although legitimate lenders may also require you to pay application, appraisal, or credit report fees, these fees are never required before the lender is identified and the application is completed. These are payments before any service, and then no service is provided—much like scams that pretend to help people with credit problems or home loans in default.

In most instances, you never receive the promised loan and either never hear from the loan company again or are later told by the "turn-down room"—a third party that denies applications for loans and other credit—that you are ineligible for the credit. Small businesses have been charged as much as several thousand dollars as an advance fee for a larger loan. Whether you are an individual or the owner of a small business, the result is the same: You do not get your money; the con artist does.

It is illegal to ask for money up front to help obtain a loan. The money must be in your hands for seven days before payment can be requested. This is the same for either a direct loan or through a third party. Get loan offers in writing, shop around, then compare promises to the written agreement. You can obtain free or low-cost credit counseling from a variety of reliable sources.

It is not always undercapitalized small business owners who are targeted by such tricksters. Recent cases have shown business-people seeking multimillion-dollar loans for ventures that were rejected by more conventional lenders and in the process losing $250,000 to $750,000 to bogus advance fees. Drawn in by the impressive executive offices and apparently affluent connections of high-flying brokers, entrepreneurs, after paying, are soon faced with delays, evasions, and excuses, followed by the disappearance of the perpetrators along with the funds collected. Occasionally a Ponzi structure needs to be established to work this scam, but fabricated word-of-mouth success stories usually do the trick.

Friends and Family

Certainly the best way to lose friends is to lend them money or borrow from them. This is absolutely true if the sum is more than an occasional twenty. So tread carefully. On the other hand, friends and family can get caught up in your new business concept and be willing to help. In fact, by one estimate more than half of all small businesses are started with money from friends and family.

There are some obvious advantages to this kind of borrowing: the cash is often readily available without a lot of paperwork, the terms are friendly, and the repayment period can be extended—sometimes way too long. The obvious drawback is that you risk friendships and family relations. If you do not repay on a timely basis, you lose trust. Nothing causes hard feelings like money.

But there is a right way to do this. Make the request a formal process, meeting with your friends or family and presenting your business plan just as though you were going to the bank. You can ask them to be investors, in which case they own part of the company and there is no loan repayment—but you will have to share the profits at some future date. If the company fails, they have lost their investment. If the company is a success, and its value increases over time, they are rewarded handsomely when the company is sold or they sell their shares and exit the business.

If you ask for a loan, make sure that there is a promissory note that stipulates the specific details of the loan, including a payment schedule, what happens if the business is sold, and what efforts will be made to keep everyone informed about the business. Simple loan documents can be purchased from several organizations, and you can even find them for free on some content-rich business sites.

Whether an equity stake or a loan, make sure the boundaries are clear about day-to-day decision making and operations. As a rule, friends and family should be passive investors or lenders unless there is some strong operational reason to include them—some special experience that will add to management's acumen. Go so far as to put this in writing; be specific about the roles everyone plays. This is a business, not a casual event. It is reasonable to have the discipline to report periodically about the status of the company—preparing financial statements such as a balance sheet and an income statement. Your family should not have to come to you to ask how their investment is going.

What happens if something goes wrong? It is important not to ignore problems. A little bit of bad news is better than a whole big mess spelled out at the last minute. If the business fails, be prepared to pay the promissory note off personally—even if it takes you years. Never borrow money from aging parents who need this cash for retirement or as their safety net—no matter how sure you are that your business will be a huge success. It is just not right to put friends and family at risk and take money they cannot really afford to invest or lend. The same advice about not using your home for collateral for a loan applies to siblings and parents. You could take out a term life or disability insurance policy and make your family member the beneficiary just in case.

Cash Strapped in the End?

After considerable effort, you may not be able to find the funding you hoped to raise or borrow. That does not mean that you should necessarily abandon your plans. But it may well mean that adjustments are necessary.

If you receive feedback from lenders, advisors, or potential investors that your plan seems unworkable or unrealistic, you have to go back to the drawing board and either adjust the original plan or start new and research other business opportunities. This kind of feedback is important and should not be dismissed outright. Some entrepreneurs have a certain tenacity, so they tend to want to ignore the bad news and plunge ahead anyway. It is difficult to generalize about this point. If the failure to fund the project is based on personal finances and not the business plan, then you need to take time to repair your credit and save more money. If the rejection is based on the fact that your ideas just do not seem workable and has nothing to do with your personal finances, you really need to reconsider some or all of your ideas.

If the plan seems good and generally accepted by outside reviewers and you have your finances in reasonable order, but you are still not able to raise all of the capital you need, you can still go forward, but scale back the operation and the plan. You could start part-time rather than full-time; learn to negotiate with suppliers or downsize the office or the number of employees. Slow the growth of your business. A common reason for failure is that a good business simply grows too quickly, outstrips its cash, and cannot meet its obligations. Growth in products and services, customers, and staff is essential but, like candy or liquor, too much of a good thing can backfire.

Resources

QuickBooks is not the only accounting software on the market, but it is clearly the best known and probably the best supported. Intuit, the publisher, allows first-time users to sample the software online for free. Naturally, there are multiple products depending on your needs—you can upgrade or buy a package specifically developed for a retail store. For more information visit http://quickbooks .intuit.com.

The peer-to-peer lenders mentioned in this chapter can be found by visiting these sites:

Lending Club (San Francisco): www.lendingclub.com
Prosper (San Francisco): www.prosper.com
Zopa (London): http://uk.zopa.com/

Entrepreneur has several free financial forms available; they are also in the business of selling forms, so not everything you need is free for the taking: www.entrepreneur.com/formnet/.

The U.S. Department of Justice provides a listing of approved credit counseling agencies by state and judicial district. You can also find agencies that conduct business in twenty-five different languages: www.justice.gov/ust/eo/bapcpa/ccde/cc_approved.htm.

FIVE

Professional Advisors

Things to know before starting a business:

▶ *Objective advice is a must.*

▶ *There are times to save money, and there are times to spend money for advice.*

▶ *Incorporation is the best means of protecting your personal resources.*

Professional Help

Throughout this book I stress the importance of having good, objective advice and assistance. In particular, there are five main types of advisors that almost every new business should have: lawyer, accountant, banker, insurance broker, and business coach. Their degree of participation in your business will vary greatly depending on the complexity and size of the business. If you engage in a part-time dog-walking business, informally structured, as an income generator in retirement and plan to keep the business as a small operation, your needs for advice are relatively small. Perhaps you hire the services of a bookkeeper at the end of the year to determine income for tax purposes, and that's about it—including not incorporating the business.

But many entrepreneurs have more ambitious plans. They start small by necessity, but their overall objective is to build a sustainable business—even if they never plan on working full-time. You cannot build such a business in a vacuum. You need professional assistance from time to time. The degree of your need is a judgment only you can make. You may speak to a lawyer once in two years, or, if you are involved in patents and extensive, complicated contracts, you may speak to one weekly.

Cost of services is an important issue. If you happen to have a close friend or relative who is an accountant or lawyer, she may give you a good deal. If you are not so fortunate, frequent use of advisors can be costly. Billing is usually by the hour, or partial hour; two hours on the phone with your lawyer can end up costing $500 or $600, conservatively.

Lawyers

A thousand jokes come across the Internet daily about lawyers; you either love them or hate them. The fact is that at some point in your business maturation you are going to need legal advice. Legal needs are in direct proportion to the size and complexity of the business. Legal needs are also in direct proportion to your business experience and acumen. It is not unreasonable for owner/managers to handle simple matters of contracts without further assistance—if they know enough.

Incorporation

Should you use a lawyer to help you incorporate? The services available online, on the surface, seem more than sufficient for the vast majority of newly formed companies. Nevertheless, entrepreneurs need and want hand-holding. A lawyer's services would be appropriate for a buyout of a large established business or a complicated partnership with large amounts of initial capital at play. Some franchise deals may require expert legal advice when starting up, particularly with review of the franchise agreement and related documents.

A *general corporation* (C) and a *limited liability company* (LLC) currently seem to be the preferred forms of business ownership. In both cases, the biggest advantage is that personal assets (home, car, investments) cannot be seized or garnished to pay off company debts, loans, or damages from a lawsuit. An LLC has the further advantage that any business losses in the early years can be used to shelter your personal income taxes, thus reducing your potential liability to the government. All of this is in sharp contrast to a sole proprietorship, a business entity without benefits of incorporation. In a sole proprietorship, there is no legal distinction between business assets and liabilities and personal assets and liabilities; the law does not recognize the sole proprietor as different from his company. This owner can receive all profits after taxes but is also exposed to unlimited liability (a lawsuit, for example). There is no corporate shell to protect the owner in case of catastrophe.

But there are more benefits to incorporation: Corporations are taxed at a lower rate than individuals, that is, sole proprietors. It is much easier to sell or transfer company assets when your company is a corporation. You can set up retirement or other qualified plans much more easily. A corporation can issue stock and raise money to build the business—an alternative to debt financing. A corporation is durable; it survives even if its shareholders, directors, or managing partner die or are disabled. Finally, corporations have their own credit rating; they are not dependent on nor do they affect the personal credit ratings of the shareholders or directors.

In the process of incorporation, articles of incorporation are filed with the secretary of state along with your corporate bylaws. Both of these documents are often boilerplate, which is why you can buy incorporation services so cheaply. Some vendors even give you a kit complete with bylaws, stock certificates, and a company seal. Finally, your company has to have a name that is different from that of any other corporation registered with the state. And each name has to have a legal ending—Inc. or LLC—to show the form of incorporation. Your corporate name does not, however, have to be your public trading name. You could register as Acme 123, LLC, but do business as The Aquarium Store.

If any or all of this makes you nervous, hire an attorney to manage the incorporation. But know that the cost will include not only the incorporation fees but also the lawyer's time. Anticipate a substantial difference between the do-it-yourself costs of incorporation and the lawyered-up version. But with the latter you are paying for service and a sense of security.

Finding and Working with a Lawyer

As with finding a dentist or a plumber, you can do an Internet search. Or you can do the prudent thing and ask for recommendations from friends, colleagues, family members, your accountant, even your insurance broker. Professions in related fields such as accounting can be a tremendous source of good information and referral—and they are happy to help. Also check with the local bar association.

Most lawyers are in private practice, with many specializing in divorce, real estate, or criminal matters. You most likely need a generalist unless you anticipate significant legal issues. You may choose to hire someone who is a business specialist, but again that really depends on the size of the business you are actually operating or the complexity of the operations and contracts you have or will enter into. The American Bar Association suggests that it is common practice to interview lawyers before engaging one. Most attorneys allow some casual time, without fee, to chat and get acquainted; some may bill for this time, so ask before you make the appointment.

As a rule of thumb, lawyers with offices in or around the business district are more expensive that those with offices elsewhere. Lawyers in large firms charge substantially higher fees than those in a small private practice. One of your first questions is about billing—not only how much but whether it is by the hour or is perhaps a monthly retainer. (You hope you won't use a lawyer often enough to make a retainer structure necessary.) And what are the payment terms? Can you pay in installments? Ask for a written fee document. What about costs such as delivery services—who pays those? Always remind yourself and your prospective counsel that you are an entrepreneur; when you get rich, he can raise his fees. When interviewing lawyers, or inquiring through a referral, ask about the kinds of experience, areas of practice, how long they have been practicing, and whether their business is primarily with individual clients or businesses.

If your lawyer is in a group practice or part of a firm, ask who would actually handle your business. It is not uncommon for a senior member to pass along basic work to a junior member or even a paralegal. Does this change the fee structure? You might be surprised that a lawyer you interview may refer you to another individual or firm, but this is not uncommon. Your business may be too small, or the lawyer you talk to may have neither the time nor the qualifications you specifically need. Don't be put off; this is standard practice.

There are two cases when an entrepreneur needs a lawyer: when buying a franchise and when buying an existing business. You absolutely need an experienced advocate to look out for your best interests and help you interpret the information (documents from due diligence or the franchise operating agreement) you receive prior to making the purchase. Your attorney should be looking at your exposure, financially and legally—what problems or liabilities will occur in the future if you buy a franchise or an existing company. The best use of a lawyer is to prevent problems, not solve them. If you are about to enter into a complex contract—for example, an offer to buy a business—it is money well spent to have your counsel review the documents and help you negotiate changes favorable to your company, and far better than asking for help to defend your performance at a later date.

If you are working with counsel to solve an existing problem, it is important to ask his opinion about the outcome. No one is clairvoyant, but if he is experienced and understands the full dimensions of the problem, he can certainly offer an educated opinion. Also, if you are being sued, or if serious financial or operating problems may result, it may be better to settle rather than fight. Pride tells you to defend your good name and business; it may be a better business decision to pay rather than fight—it may cost substantially less. The lesson is always to cut your losses when necessary. Being right may make you feel better, but it may not be good for business.

You may want to think of your lawyer as your silent business partner—and the same is true for all of your advisors. Be honest about problems, actions taken, and your views on certain matters. Also, understand that the more work you can do, the less the lawyer has to do and bill you for. There are dozens of documents and pieces of information you can prepare ahead of time to make a process work better and faster. Information needs to be timely. If something changes, make sure your lawyer knows about it right away. This is particularly important when the matter is about resolving business disputes.

Accountants

The role of an accountant varies hugely depending, again, on the complexity of your business. There are many different kinds of accountants, from simple bookkeeper or tax preparer to accounting associate to certified public accountant (CPA). There are also accounting specialists by industry, by function (managerial versus taxes), by public company or private company, among others.

Returning to our dog-walking company, this owner may never need the services of an accountant—even for tax purposes. In theory this entrepreneur could prepare his own taxes, since he is probably a sole proprietor, and income generated from his dog-walking business is added to other earned income for tax purposes. A simple receipts ledger or even a stand-alone software accounting package could easily take care of his needs.

But let's assume our dog walker plans to expand to a full-blown service with staff, an office, a substantial client base, and marketing and promotional costs and also expects to add grooming and other services to the business over time. At some point, he is a candidate for a good accountant. His needs are still not complicated, but he will require help—particularly filing tax returns and perhaps preparing financial statements for bankers and possibly investors. Once again, with a good accounting software package such as QuickBooks, he can manage much of the monthly activity—invoicing, posting collections, paying staff, making quarterly tax deposits, paying bills—and thus keep costs down.

In such a case, an accountant can serve as your mentor and advisor—teaching you how and when to do various tasks and helping you work on your financial planning and cash-flow needs. Once a year, outside of tax time, you could ask for advice on credit, collections, cost reductions, tax minimization, and a host of matters. If the business grows substantially, you may turn over many of these functions (paying bills, posting invoices) to a staff member and retain the accountant to handle more sophisticated matters.

But it is not just what the accountant does that is so important, it is what the accountant knows. Accountants understand businesses and their growing pains. They are especially valuable in smoothing the link between your personal and business finances—ensuring that you get every benefit you can from the business while protecting your personal finances.

Similar to a lawyer, an accountant is particularly important when you buy another business (or a franchise); you want experienced eyes looking at the previous business, asking about patterns of disbursements, looking for gaps in funding or efforts to hide appropriations of payments. You need the experience to see if the "books have been cooked"—making the business look better than it actually is. Having a certified (licensed) accountant at your side when you visit your banker can make a big difference, too. The banker knows that a professional has prepared and reviewed the financial statements of your company and that they are free from error or fraud.

One of the biggest roles an accountant will play is helping you with year-end tax preparation and ongoing tax planning. Just as important, you want an accountant at your side in the event of a tax audit or a review by the bank's auditors. (If the loan amount is substantial, it is common policy for the bank to arrange for an annual audit/review to verify the financial statements you submit.) At some point in the maturation of your business, you may need independent auditors to actually conduct annual audits; this is customary in larger businesses, to satisfy not only regulators and government agencies but the bank and any shareholders as well.

Finding an accountant is similar to finding a lawyer. Review these general principles:

> ▶ What are your needs? You should seek an accountant who meets your needs. Are you looking for tax compliance and planning? Looking for an audit, review, or compilation? Do you need a business valuation?

> ▶ Ask for referrals. Once you know what you need, seek out referrals from others you trust. Ask friends, business associates, and other professionals. But proceed with caution. An accountant who is good for someone else is not necessarily a proper fit for you.

> ▶ Ask specifically about the fee structure and what you might typically be billed for basic services and any other special reports you may need. As always, get it in writing.

> ▶ Ask questions. When you find one or two people who appear to match your needs, start asking questions. Make a list of the matters that are important to you. Such questions can address education, experience, specialties, and business philosophy. Ask how they have assisted others in similar circumstances (though

an accountant can answer only in generalities and not about specific clients).

▶ Assess communication and comfort. Now that you feel confident that this person is appropriate for your specific circumstances, evaluate your comfort level with him. How does he communicate? Is it high-level technical talk, or does he lay things out in an organized, understandable format? Does he prefer e-mail, phone, or in-person meetings? One way to gauge his communication skills is by the manner in which he responds to your questions. Is he irritated and short? Or is he professional and enthusiastic about having you as a potential client?

Bankers

Although bankers have traditionally been thought of as adversaries, or at least people you need to keep happy, in fact they can be a tremendous resource. As you can see in other chapters of this book, the primary function of the banking relationship is to build a borrowing base and a capital structure for your company. But your banker can serve a variety of roles other than just approving lines of credit.

The bank itself has a variety of services, all for a fee, of course, from investments to cash management services. Even if you do not or cannot take advantage of these services, meeting with the banker on a regular basis can provide insight into the economic climate, locally and nationally. Bankers are in a position to make significant introductions, such as to the president of the bank, other bank customers who could become your clients, vendors, and even possible investors. And then there are contractors, con-sultants, distributors, prospective employees, technology ser-vices—on and on.

Insurance Brokers

It may come as a bit of surprise that you can think of your friendly insurance agent as one of your advisors. In fact, insurance agents can be extremely important in one key area: risk management of both your personal and business assets. Risk management is all about managing uncertainty. Obviously, some risks can be con-trolled, others not. But you can be protected financially or opera-tionally from some hazards (fire, death of a key employee). There are several overall ways to manage risk: You can transfer the risk to another party; you can avoid the risk; you can try to reduce the effects of the risk; or you can accept some of the risk as an inevi-table part of business and life.

Roughly speaking, risk management for smaller businesses falls into three broad categories: legal, physical, and financial. As soon as you open your business, all three types of risk exist. The trick is to identify and quantify the degree of risk you have and to put together a strategy to manage it. This is an area of the business development that is often ignored with the famous last words "It will never happen to me. I will not have a fire or flood; no one will sue me."

Risks come from every direction, and, again, some can be con-trolled, and others not. Some are reasonably insurable, others not. Imagine, for instance, that you run a chain of three retail stores, fast-food takeaway stores that are open late at night. Almost all of your help are part-time students. What are some of your risks?

Business risk: The economy tanks, and people limit or
terminate their fast-food consumption.

Accident risk: An employee or customer gets hurt on your
premises.

Operational risk: You serve tainted food by mistake, lose
your license, and get sued.

Physical risk: Fire, flood, wind, or water (leaking pipes)
damage occurs.

Disability: You get hurt and cannot manage the business.

The business risk is almost impossible to handle or minimize; you
cut your losses by closing one or all locations and selling the businesses, or you spend the capital you have saved to ride out the hard
time. All the rest can be managed (not eliminated because someone
can always sue) by various kinds of insurance.

Take another example. You run a small accounting firm with
a partner and three employees. Your partner is the front man: he
meets and greets customers, calls on accounts, and is the face to
the business. What are your risks?

Key-employee risk: Your partner dies or is disabled.

Failure-to-perform risk: You fail to file taxes on time, and a
client is hit with big fines and penalties.

Business risk: Your biggest client goes out of business.

Operational risk: Your computer melts down, and you lose
client data.

The one loss you probably cannot manage in any way is the loss
of a key client, unless you saw it coming. The other risks could at
least be mitigated through key-man life insurance; an errors-and-
omissions policy in cases of failure to perform (very expensive

insurance); and outsourcing computer services so that you have adequate backup. In the latter case, no insurance is involved, but you pay for an outside service to prevent business loss or interruptions.

One could make the point that all business is risk, but taken on freely with the expectation of a substantial reward personally and financially. Using your insurance broker or agent to help you manage risk, thus serving as one of your key outside advisors, is a good plan for most small businesses. As the business becomes larger, the risks increase, and greater attention needs to be paid to a variety of insurance, annuity, and other schemes that can help reduce risk exposure.

Businesspeople often think of insurance agents as salespeople and nothing more. In fact, they are trained and can bring a level of sophistication to your business that may not be obvious on the surface. Invite your broker or agent to be part of your team. Listen to her and ask questions about the kinds of insurance and protection available. You may need nothing in the first year or two of operation—or the minimum. But there will come a time when you cannot afford to replace assets and key personnel—in short, when you must afford to take the necessary precautions to protect your business.

One form of risk management is a business-interruption policy, which, in the case of fire or a major catastrophe, helps you set up and run your business from a different location and pays to replace some of the lost income until you are fully operational. This and errors-and-omissions insurance are both expensive but effective risk management tools.

A good broker is going to not only advise you about the types of insurance to be considered but help you formulate a level of coverage that is appropriate for the business at any given time.

Simple kinds of insurance, like term life insurance and coverage on the company car, are easy to shop for and can be done on the Internet. In other cases, you want to understand exactly what you are buying and whether there are holes in the coverage. The insurance company is not in the business of paying out just because you say so. There are always exclusions and exceptions. Get your broker to explain, in writing, what you are buying and how the costs compare from one company to the next. An annual review of your risk management needs is probably sufficient.

Business Coaches

This profession, and in fact this service, has grown substantially in the past ten years. Analogous to an athletic coach, on which the concept is modeled, the business coach provides objective information and analysis of your business strategies and tactics. The relationship, although paid, is one of mentor, analyst, and critic all rolled up into one. What you are not hiring is a friend. The only way to use this service effectively is to expose your business and your personal management style to an open critique.

It is important to understand that this is strictly a business relationship, with a bit of a pep rally feel. The coach's role should be to critique, suggest, help plan, organize, motivate, and encourage. To use this process effectively, you have to be willing to share reports and other documents, discuss your management style, explain your operations fully, and allow an objective person to comment and suggest change—if it is needed. The trick is to not take the discussion personally, and to have a coach who can respond to bad news without being abrasive or insulting.

What does a business coach bring to your business? First of all, as already mentioned, she brings objectivity. Business coaches are not paid employees; they are not you; they are not wedded to the original business plan or business concept; they are apart from all operations. They come with a strong background—either in business or in the processes related to management; they have and should demonstrate wisdom. Business coaches are also innovators; they see and can connect elements that might at first not seem related. They also have the ability to make complex matters simple by breaking them down to their simplest elements. As important, they are agents of change and are there to challenge your management as well as the business practices in place.

Many people put up a shingle and call themselves business coaches. Like all of the other advisors discussed, you will find a coach only after some trial and error. Get the usual referrals from friends, business associates, family members, and colleagues. Check with your other advisors: bankers, accountants, lawyers, and insurance brokers. Follow the same process. Interview. Ask for referrals, what organizations they belong to, what kinds of business they specialize in (or perhaps size), how they charge. Also know the limits; can you just call up and talk, or do you need a formal appointment? Will the coach come on-site to see you and your business in operation? No one size fits all.

It is extremely important to set rules on both sides. Is the coach's role to listen to you moan about the state of your business, or to effect change? The coach has personal limits and space as well: other clients, a right to regular office hours, and a right to be paid on a timely basis. In short, business coaches (like all your advisors) have lives beyond you and your business. They also have the right to fire you if the relationship does not work out. They may want your fees, but there are limits if nothing changes within the organization or your management style does not mature.

In short, a management coach is highly recommended, especially in the first year or two of business operations. You may easily outgrow this relationship and the need for this expertise; you may need to find other advisors instead, such as an accountant or a full-blown consulting specialist to help fill the gaps.

Resources

A quick Internet search for "do-it-yourself incorporation" will turn up dozens of sites, such as www.nolo.com and www.legalzoom.com. Most of these groups compete on price, and they all have very similar programs. You can also buy a variety of forms and business kits to help you with employee and general management issues. Again, this kind of content is inexpensive and generally well done.

Not surprisingly, business coaches have their own professional organization, Worldwide Association of Business Coaches, founded in 1997—which tells you just how new the profession really is. For further information and how to find a coach, visit www.wabccoaches.com.

SIX

Starting Up Part-Time, Moving to Full-Time

Things to know before starting a business:

▶ *Starting part-time can be the smart route to full-time.*

▶ *Conflicts of interest with your current employer are a risk not to ignore.*

▶ *Time management is more critical than ever.*

▶ *You need support for your venture from family, friends, and colleagues*

The Part-Time Advantage

Much of the focus of this book is managing risk—no matter the specific kind of risk under consideration. Risk management is about improving your chances of building a successful business, by whatever definition of success you choose. If you plan to start a new business (as opposed to buying an existing company), there are excellent reasons to start part-time and move to full-time employment as your company grows. (The assumption is that there are very few part-time businesses for sale, and those that are would be difficult to value.)

There are some specific advantages of starting part-time:

- You may be able to retain your current employment, with salary and benefits.
- You reduce substantially the amount of money required to launch the business.
- You have the leisure to experiment and tinker not only with your business concept but with the actual running of the business.
- You put much less pressure on yourself and your personal finances, since your cash-flow needs are smaller.
- Part-time businesses are less complicated.
- You can walk away from a part-time business far more easily than a full-time operation.
- You can run the business from your home, often without a huge investment in equipment and inventory.
- Many part-time businesses can be Internet based.

Starting Off from a Full-Time Base

It should be clearly understood that anyone at any time in life can start a business. Students, active retirees, and the unemployed begin enterprises on a regular basis, with full expectation that they will succeed. However, one group of individuals has, in my view, the best chance of success: those individuals who are actively employed, with salary and benefits. Specifically, it is the combination of full-time employment and starting a business on the side that can be particularly attractive. The practical reality is that it is hard to start a business, full-time or part-time, without financial security. The focus of this chapter thus narrows in recognition that it simply is easier to start a business while you have income and some degree of security.

Once you establish the premise of a full-time job in the background, the drawbacks of starting up your own part-time business become clear:

- Essentially, you are working two jobs.
- You may be tempted to work on your new business during regular business hours.
- Your company may have a policy against outside employment.
- You may be tempted to use assets (office supplies or information) that belong to your employer, which is unethical.
- Your new business may be a distraction, so much so that your performance suffers at your full-time job.
- Your business may compete with your current employer.
- Working two jobs takes away from the quality of your life, allowing less time for family and friends.

These points are elaborated in the rest of this section; some of them, to be sure, are also generally applicable to anyone starting part-time, in any circumstance.

Conflict of Interest

One of the biggest problems you face is potential conflict of interest. A conflict of interest exists when any individual has competing personal or professional interests, and it is best to define conflict of interest here in the most inclusive way possible in order to be the most conservative, that is, minimize risk. The simplest case is when you are employed in some capacity and then start a part-time business that is in direct competition with your employer—while you are still employed, receiving wages and benefits. A conflict of interest can exist even if there is no legal issue involved; there are still ethical issues to consider.

Conflict of interest is more than just directly competing; it can include using your employer's resources, physical property, time (on the job), Internet (when you should be doing something else), and so forth. Many people would judge this as acceptable behavior; but if your supervisor or manager got wind of this kind of activity, it could be cause for dismissal.

It is important to review any documents you signed at the time of your employment. Some organizations have strict rules about running a second business or even having a part-time job—without permission. Remember, most people are employees at will—meaning that they do not have a contract to protect them in case of an employment dispute. They can simply be fired. Look also at the employee handbook. If there is still doubt about your employer's position, speak to someone in human resources with the assurance that your inquiry will not be used against you.

It is difficult to be objective about a situation that may be a conflict of interest. It can easily be a slippery slope, where rationalization and poor judgment take the place of objectivity and fairness. You only took a few office supplies, or you spent just a few minutes on the phone working your business. It is easy to move from the small activities to spending a good part of your day working for yourself. And, of course, there is the pragmatic issue that getting fired is going to set back your business plans—perhaps indefinitely.

No matter how hard you try to keep your small business to yourself, you will be discovered by another worker. Someone overhears a phone conversation, or you leave documents at the copy machine. You are starting part-time specifically to ensure that you have an income during the early stages of the business. And though income needs to be protected, benefits such as health insurance can be just as critical. So don't get fired. You need to make an important decision: keep your personal plans and business activities out of the workplace.

One final note: If you are planning a business that may compete with your current employer, now or in the future, be particularly careful. You can open yourself up to a lawsuit and damages. One extreme example involved a middle manager who took an employer's database, left the company, and started a business using this list. The business was opened, offices leased, equipment purchased, and marketing begun—with the aid of an investor. A substantial amount of money was put up to get the new business running. Within three months, the entrepreneur's former employer sued and won money damages for the use of its customer lists. This individual was forced to return a bonus and termination benefits, the business was closed, and the investor and the owner lost a substantial amount of money.

Not only do you want to stay out of conflict, real or perceived, with your employer, you should recognize the importance of your full-time employment—even if you hate the job. Your current employment is the key to surviving the first six months or even the first year in your new business. Nothing puts greater pressure on the small-business owner than not having income to support the family and lifestyle while starting up.

Time Management

Time is not on your side when you take the plunge to start a business. In fact, time management (along with financial management) is one of the most important issues you face. If you spend all of your evenings and all weekend working your new business, you will come back to your full-time employer exhausted and unable to perform your regular duties satisfactorily. This will be a quick tip-off to the boss that something is going on.

This same pattern will destroy your personal and family life. It is hard enough to work a full-time job, build a business, and have angry or frustrated family members constantly complaining that you are never available for family outings, a movie, or vacation. Further, it is not healthy; you are putting too much pressure on yourself, and you will not be able to sustain that kind of pace.

Work out a schedule for the week and stick to it. Perhaps you work for four evenings from 7:00 to 9:00 and a full day on Saturday. Don't work holidays; don't work on days promised to your spouse or family; take one full day off from both your employment and your small business. To make this work, you have to be disciplined—both ways. If it is time to work and there is work to do, don't put it off. If you have more work than you can complete that day or evening, stop at your regular time and start again at your regular time. Admittedly, in the beginning this may be difficult, because there will be so much to do, but as time progresses set your schedule and stick to it.

Time management means that you have a plan for the time you spend in your new office. Set priorities, even if they are unpleasant, and stick to your scheduled work. Do the things that *need* doing. It is easy to decide to make some small changes to your website or rearrange the office furniture, neither of which is going to generate significant revenue. Your focus should be on marketing, sales, collections, customer service, and those tasks that generate cash. It takes discipline to work in the evening after you have already worked a full day, spent time preparing dinner, and managed some household chores.

Many organizations have flex time, which allows you to start earlier (or later) than the traditional eight or nine o'clock in the morning, as long as all team members are together for the majority of the day. If you are a morning person, you can begin earlier, get home earlier, and have some productive home-business hours. Or you can do the opposite: Start early in the morning at your office place of business; it may be easier to establish customer contacts. If flex time is not an option, the beauty of the contemporary high-tech world is that you can leave your place of employment, find a park bench or Internet café, and with a cell phone and laptop or tablet conduct business for 45 minutes to an hour. You can answer e-mails, make calls, prepare and send proposals, help customers. It is amazing what you can do in a short time.

As the business grows, you may need a part-time employee to help with everyday work. This assumes that you are still at the very early stages and cannot manage without the income and benefits from your employer—or are reluctant to do so. Your employee can be a remote one—never actually present in your home office. You can direct your office phone to the employee for part of the day; anyone can go in and check for messages and e-mail. You can meet once a week to go over other work or assignments that you want done during business hours as well. Often the cost for such help is minimal; such office assistants work for themselves, so in most environments you do not have to do tax reporting and filing on their behalf. But remember that managing any employee means being able to manage yourself—it means that you have the discipline and maturity to plan high-quality work that will build your business.

Relationships Management and Building Support

Whether you start full-time or part-time, whether with a secure job in your pocket or not, the success of your business is directly based on being able to manage the various relationships—personal, business, and familial. First and foremost, you want family support—your spouse or significant other and the children (if they are old enough to participate generally). If the business comes before family and friends, you will be isolated, divorced, lonely, miserable, or all of the above. The key is balance and building support from the beginning.

Be realistic and open about how much time it is going to take if you start a part-time business and retain full-time employment. Some spouses may be willing to participate in some fashion—perhaps act as a backup when you are not available. Many couples do not want to work together or build a business together; there simply is too great a risk of conflict and ruining a perfectly good relationship.

If you have a family and a spouse, you need to sit down and set up the parameters; seek their emotional as well as financial support for what you are doing. Set up a real benchmark—six months to one year later—to decide if the business is a success or at least is going in the right direction. Remember, you also have friends and extended family who need and want your time and attention. That can be a lot to manage. Anticipate the problem and set about dividing up responsibilities in light of the new reality. Poker night may be out, but going to see family or friends on Sunday may be a good outlet and satisfying for everyone.

Relationship management is equally important if you have partners or silent investors. You have to decide from the beginning who is doing what and who is ultimately responsible for final decisions. Someone has to be boss. Furthermore, investors and others need and want information about the status of the company—sales, inventory, cash management, strategy, and changes in the business plan. Set aside time once a month and have complete, understandable documents ready when you meet.

One relationship that may be useful is someone to be your backup while you are traveling, on vacation, or sick and cannot attend to the new business as you normally would. Once again, a laptop and cell phone can assist, as in taking a few minutes a day while traveling to handle essential business. You have other options: a part-time employee, a spouse (with some obvious limitations), a partner, an investor, or a friend you can train. Your professional advisors could help in a pinch, but that might end up costing more than you are making. Business continuity is a real problem, and it can be a real drag. You want to golf but cannot go because you have a business to run.

Tips for Starting

Especially if you are working for other businesses or sophisticated consumers, appearances are everything. Have a dedicated e-mail address and mailing address for your business. The same is true for the phone; use one phone account as a dedicated business line. If your primary place of business is your home and your business requires you to meet clients, try to arrange it at their place of business. If you can't, you can rent office space by the hour. Perhaps a friend or vendor can lend you a conference room on occasion. Offer to pay for the use rather than expect it for free.

If you are using a room in your home as a business, learn what tax breaks there are and take advantage of them—and follow the tax law scrupulously. Some people have a general fear of audits or fines. But if you follow the rules, you should have no problems. In most cases the home office has to be dedicated completely to a business—not part of the family room where kids can play video games or the family can surf the Internet on your business computer.

When, and if, you make the transition to full-time business owner, it is important that you avoid physical and social isolation, which can come easily, especially if you are working at home or on the computer all day (as opposed to working retail). This can be devastating over time—your only human contact may be e-mail. Make a point of meeting clients, friends, and former colleagues for lunch or coffee. Call as well as e-mail. You need human interaction; otherwise you risk being isolated and unproductive.

Time to Test Your Concept

Of all the advantages of starting part-time, the ability to test your concept (market plan) is certainly the most important. You can find out quickly that your business model is just not right and thereby cut your losses and go on to try something else. This is especially critical if you are trying to keep a full-time job as well.

There are other times when the business model is right, but you just do not like the business. Take the example of a technically sophisticated person who has decided that he can make a nice income on the side solving computer and Internet problems for consumers. It is the perfect business in that little is required for start-up; it matches the owner's skill set perfectly; and the work is done at someone's home office, so there is no need for an office beyond a simple one in the basement. Further, the owner finds that he can usually stop at a client's house on the way home from work or on Saturday mornings.

After six or so months, this entrepreneur has had no difficulty finding clients through his local church bulletin, Internet posts, a variety of social media, and referrals. And the pace is right—one or two clients a week works out well. What the owner finds awkward is the social interaction and trying to explain technical problems to unsophisticated people. He finds the experience frustrating because of the human interaction and demanding, whining complaints of some clients. Had he struck out on his own, full-time, he would have had a rude and expensive awakening—finding that, even though the model was right, it was not a business he enjoyed. He just did not like dealing with the general public.

One test of your business model is how customers take the fact that you are only a part-time entrepreneur. Do they take you seriously? If your business is soft science such as pet services or landscape consulting, you would not meet much resistance. On the other hand, if you are directing your efforts to serving business—say consulting or coaching—will people perceive you as a real businessperson who can fulfill their needs? Such a perception problem is always difficult for small businesses. And, of course, there is the issue of availability: can you see a business client during the day while working full-time?

Transition to a Full-Time Business

There can be any number of strong motives for starting your business part-time—all of them practical—from saving money to testing your business model. But ultimately, in your planning and thinking, you need to decide if the part-time business is a platform for going full-time or just a means to bring in extra income while you continue with your day job.

You should have made this decision, one way or the other, when you wrote the business plan. That does not mean that you cannot change your theory of the business after experimentation and time on the job. If your original plan was to start the business for extra income and you never planned to work at it full-time, you could ultimately decide that it is too difficult to work two jobs, and you have to make a decision: abandon the part-time business altogether or take the plunge and work full-time for yourself.

Your experiences as a part-time entrepreneur will, of course, influence your ultimate decision; that's what testing your plan means. You may find it frustrating that you cannot grow the business or have to rely on part-time help because you are fully employed. You may find after six to ten months that you could live off the income the business provides if you devoted your full time to it. The extra income from the part-time business may have helped you get your personal finances in rock-solid shape, allowing you to move to full-time with less risk and greater financial security.

If the decision is to move full-time into your business, you need to plan for that transition carefully. But the best advice is not to rush to judgment too quickly. Before you give your employer notice, you may want to take advantage of company-sponsored benefits. Get a complete physical while still on the company plan; private insurance is very expensive. Obviously, if there are health issues, postpone indefinitely your plans to be a full-time entrepreneur.

Make sure that any pension or other plans in which you are vested are not lost because you leave six months too soon. Perhaps if you stay just a bit longer your benefits will increase, making it worth your while to plan your departure from your employer differently than first anticipated. One excellent strategy before you leave your employer is to take out a home equity line of credit, assuming that you qualify and your property is not underwater. Often it is difficult to do this as a small-business owner; as an employee, assuming you have good credit, it is much easier to do. Having a line of credit to draw from in the first two years would be invaluable. Give yourself plenty of time to work through the process. It can take longer than you think, especially if credit is tight or lending standards are strict. This is also an excellent time to pay down or pay off your outstanding loans and credit card balances. Minimal debt would take the pressure off you as you start full-time in your new business.

Resources

A quick Internet search of part-time businesses will bring up a load of good and not-so-good sites for your review. Here are several worth looking at.

Franchises

www.entrepreneur.com/parttimefranchises
This site is essentially a series of ads for various franchises. Click on any of the tabs, and it will tell you how much money is needed, whether you can run it from home, and if this is a candidate for part-timers.

www.franchisesolutions.com/part-time-businesses.cfm
Similar to the previous site, this quick information is more exten-sive, and you can customize your search by investment, industry, and location.

Business Ideas

www.entrepreneur.com/startingabusiness/businessideas/
article64720.html
This is a handy list of twenty-five ideas for part-time businesses—everything from antiques to yoga instructor.

Part-Time Businesses for Sale

www.businessnation.com/businesses_for_sale/
part_time_businesses.html
This site offers information about existing businesses that are for sale. Some may require full time and so might not be appropriate if you plan to keep your current job.

SEVEN

Hiring and Firing Basics

Things to know before starting a business:

▶ *Planning is critical before your hire.*

▶ *The hiring process must be simple, efficient, and, especially, legal.*

▶ *There are many alternatives to full-time employees: part-time, independent contractors, even partners.*

▶ *Job offers should be clear, in writing, and include a full job description.*

The Challenge to Get It Right

Whether you have started a business from scratch, purchased a franchise, or taken over an existing business with many employees, the challenge of hiring and firing legally and ethically is just that—a challenge. Most small and new businesses do not have professional human resource people on staff; the companies are just too small and cannot afford such specialization. The burden for employment and hiring expertise falls on you, the owner, whether you want it or not.

There are certain broad principles that govern best practices in employment. Never mind that some states have specific laws and regulations governing hiring, firing, compensation, health insurance, retirement plans, union rules, work rules, and other matters too numerous to mention. The goal of this chapter is not to make you a personnel specialist in ten minutes; you can read many fine books devoted entirely to hiring policy and practice. There are also numerous consultancies designed specifically to assist entrepreneurial companies, and the U.S. Department of Labor has devoted a website to the subject. The goal here is to introduce the crucial principles of employment.

Best practices in employment are governed by common sense and the general principles of fairness and ethical behavior. Take the high road in all matters related to hiring, and employment will always pay off. An employer-employee relationship that is built on mistrust (legal or not) will ultimately be expensive. Trained employees will quit, leaving holes in your business structure; disgruntled employees may sue over real or imagined violations of the law, and this can be terribly expensive; employees will not recommend your company to other qualified candidates, and you will not get the level of expertise you hope for.

Hiring qualified candidates is expensive and time consuming. It takes effort and perseverance to find and retain high-quality employees. But why bother, you say; your business is a fast-food operation, and you can always find employees for minimum wage. You can take this approach, but if you quantify the costs of hiring, firing, advertising, interviewing, checking backgrounds, and training, you will find that this approach is much more expensive and exhausting than taking the time to find strong candidates and being willing to pay a bit more.

Whether you have two employees or two hundred, certain overriding principles should influence you staffing decisions:

- Understand that your hiring and personnel decisions affect people's lives; be fair and reasonable in compensation, working conditions, and workloads.
- Know why you are hiring and the role that this person will play in your business. Even the smallest companies should write and use job descriptions.
- Take your time (within reason) and evaluate several qualified candidates for a job before making a decision.
- Hiring the wrong person in a small company is exponentially worse for business and morale than hiring the same wrong person in a large organization.
- Don't be afraid to seek advice; ask other employees to meet and interview candidates. Your business coach or a consultant can be a huge help when you are hiring.
- Think long and hard about hiring a relative or friend. Some spouses can work wonderfully together; most don't.
- Don't fill a job. Hire an employee.

Planning Is the Best Practice

Use the same discipline in planning your employment needs as you did developing your business concept and writing a business plan.

Best practice in hiring is putting your plan on paper and quantifying criteria when possible. Making assumptions without the financial facts is meaningless. Ask yourself some of these questions before even posting a job ad:

- ▸ What positions do you need filled and by when?
- ▸ How much can you really afford to pay? (Include the costs of benefits and mandatory government programs like unemployment insurance.)
- ▸ How high do sales have to grow before you add additional staff?
- ▸ Can your company maintain sales levels to cover the financial commitment?
- ▸ Would part-time workers be better than full-time?
- ▸ Would an independent contractor be better than an employee?
- ▸ Do you have sufficient resources to support the new hire—work space, phone, computer, tools, uniforms, work space? (Don't underestimate the indirect costs associated with a new employee; the money adds up quickly.)
- ▸ Do you know exactly what your new employee is supposed to do? What you expect once the employee is trained?
- ▸ Who will do the training?

Every one of these questions has an indirect or direct cost associated with it.

Understanding the level, experience, or sophistication of a future employee is important. Do you need an experienced marketing manager, or are you strong in this field and can train a newly minted college graduate and thus save a good deal of money? Will this employee supervise others? (Be careful here: an inexperienced manager in a small company can be explosive.) How important are technical skills such as computing or basic accounting?

Exhibit 7-1 allows you to quantify your decisions about the qualifications of your ideal candidate. Score the importance of each criterion, with 1 meaning unimportant and 9 meaning essential, and add them up. The higher your total score, the more qualified a person needs to be and, it follows logically, more expensive to hire and maintain.

EXHIBIT 7-1 ▸ **Needs Assessment**

Has college degree	1	3	5	7	9
Must have previous experience	1	3	5	7	9
Can work independently	1	3	5	7	9
Has worked in same industry	1	3	5	7	9
Has strong computer skills	1	3	5	7	9
Has direct management experience	1	3	5	7	9
Is financially literate	1	3	5	7	9
Can be promoted	1	3	5	7	9
Is mature for age	1	3	5	7	9
Has strong communication skills	1	3	5	7	9
Other requirements	1	3	5	7	9

Total Score _____

Finding the Right Person for the Job

Small businesses have some strong advantages but also many significant disadvantages when it comes to finding and hiring good employees. The smaller the business, the more difficult the challenge, unless you are willing to give up significant equity or make key employees owners in some capacity—perhaps even in an equal partnership.

On the one hand, there can be a good deal of enthusiasm for working at a small company. Employees gain vast amounts of experience that they would not normally get when compartmentalized in a department in a large organization. A small work environment allows everyone to learn from the owner/manager and other key employees. Team members get exposure to marketing and financial information that normally would not be in their purview.

There is general excitement and enthusiasm to participate in a company where an employee can grow professionally and financially as the company grows. Being on the ground floor, with all the expectations associated with this kind of experience, can be a strong motivator for employees to make sacrifices in salary, job title, and benefits. An entrepreneurial environment may have the right feel for some people—those who thrive on a less-structured, less-staid work experience, often giving time beyond the usual forty hours per week. Younger, less encumbered workers without families, big mortgages, and other responsibilities can more readily manage the transition to a small company.

The arguments against joining a smaller company are legion. Consider some of the reasons people give for not responding to recruitment or accepting employment:

- ▸ Risk of failure is substantially higher.
- ▸ It seems like a step back in career path and professional development.
- ▸ Small companies cannot compete on salary and benefits.

▸ Family and financial obligations make the risk higher.

▸ The environment is too small.

▸ Operating budgets are severely limited.

▸ There are few support staff.

▸ Working conditions and environment are cramped and of poor quality—perhaps even shabby.

▸ Candidates are overqualified for the position.

▸ Limited benefits are offered to employees.

Should the negatives overwhelm you? No. You need to formulate your recruitment strategy and not be in a rush to fill a position. Most of the online job sites cost money, which you may not be able to afford. But there are dozens of local sites, such as Craigslist, which cost much less and appeal to different employee segments. Posting on college bulletin boards as well as through industry groups improves your chances of getting qualified resumes.

Use college placement services if you are willing to hire someone with little experience; however, you may find that recent alumni also register on these lists, such as former students who have been out for a few years, have some experience, but are searching for new employment and new challenges. If you personally or your company is using social media, particularly LinkedIn, these are ideal for getting the word out that you have an open position. With the high unemployment in today's market, you should have no difficulty attracting a pool of qualified candidates.

Word-of-mouth advertising is absolutely one of the best ways to find qualified people. If you have prepared a short job description (and you should), you can e-mail it to friends, family, former colleagues, vendors and suppliers, your business coach, other advisors, and your many business contacts. Post the job on your company intranet to see if qualified candidates emerge from your own employee pool, no matter how small; your employees may know someone who is looking for work and is qualified for the job. It is never a good idea to post salary, or even a range.

An alternative, if you can afford it, is to use a professional placement service or head hunter. The odds are good that such services will work well, but they tend to focus their attention on larger clients, who come to them often or are on retainer. A one-time search request is neither efficient nor profitable for a placement firm. A variation on this theme is to hire part-time people through a temp agency. These temporary hires often emerge as qualified full-time employees; naturally, expect to pay a fee to the agency if you end up hiring one of its people.

The Correct Way to Hire

What follows are some of the specifics of the actual hiring process. Fairness and decency should dictate your decision making. If you have never hired someone, ask your business coach or other advisor for help. One of the advisors may even take an active role in reviewing resumes and interviewing candidates.

The Law

No matter what jurisdiction you live in, there are basic laws and court rulings that protect the rights of both employers and employees. Some very small companies are not under these hiring mandates, but as a basic rule, to protect yourself when hiring, assume that there are legal restrictions on the kinds of statements you can make and questions you can ask.

Rule 1: Ask only employment-related questions. Candidates' personal lives (with the exception of recreational drug use) have little if anything to do with their ability to function in the workplace. You are interested only in whether a person can do the job, has the background and experience to work, and will fit in with your company and team concept.

Rule 2: Absolutely avoid any discussion of racial or marital background, age, gender, nationality, birthplace, disabilities, family status (pregnant or not), or anything that even smacks of any of these topics. Focus only on qualifications.

Rule 3: If you are unsure what the law requires, hire a professional to guide you.

Rule 4: Put everything in writing—all agreements, employment applications, offers, contracts, special accommodations—anything and everything related to the employment process. If a situation goes bad in the future, e-mails and oral agreements have substantially less weight than solid written correspondence.

Résumés, Résumés, and More Résumés

You posted your job qualifications for a new position, and you are now deluged with résumés—so many, in fact, that it is a real burden to go through them all. You can screen a large number of résumés by breaking down the task into these steps:

1. Examine the quality of the résumé. Look for basic items, such as spelling and grammatical errors.

2. Look for educational level and background. If you require a college degree and candidates do not have a degree, set these aside. Although they may not be candidates for this job, they may be appropriate for other current and future open positions.

3. Review employment history and work summary. If they seem to match your needs, put them aside for further evaluation.

4. Look for gaps in the employment history or inconsistencies in credentials. Don't discard these necessarily, for there could be very legitimate reasons for being out of work for a period of time, especially in the current labor market. But be careful.

5. Look for results, performance indicators that might separate one or two candidates from the rest. Perhaps a candidate increased sales in her territory by 30 percent over two years; she goes to the top.

6. By this point, you have probably reduced the stack of résumés by 75 percent—or more. Set the qualified 25 percent aside, go on with other duties, and go back to the resumes later in the day or the next day. Take the time to get a fresh perspective.

7. Settle down and make notes on each of the remaining resumes—what is good, what might be of concern, and how well each individual matches your job description and employment needs. In the end of this session, you will have narrowed the number down to three or four résumés.

8. Get others' opinions or advice on the remaining few candidates. Another manager, a business coach, an employment consultant all can be used to evaluate the

résumés you have decided are qualified. Have everyone rank your candidates based on their perceptions of the qualifications outlined in the resume.

A Phone Interview

It is common for employers to telephone candidates and engage them in general conversation about their qualifications before setting up a personal interview. The phone interview is not the place to make a decision, but rather to weed out anyone who does not or cannot discuss their qualifications vis-à-vis their submitted resumes. You will know within a minute or two whether personal experience and written qualifications match.

A phone interview need not last more than fifteen minutes. When you reach the candidate on the phone, introduce yourself and explain the reason you are calling, Be clear and precise. Assume that the candidate has submitted more than one resume to various potential employers and may not even recall the details of your posting. Ask if this is a good time to talk. (Smart candidates will always say no, then use some time to refine their phone presentation, do further research online about your company, and generally get ready for the interview.)

In fact, they may be at work or commuting and not in a good position to talk to you. Be sensitive that, if you did call during working hours, the candidate may have to ask for a different time to speak to you. Schedule a firm time, telling each candidate that you will need fifteen minutes—no more. This is a simple process, and you don't want to spend a lot of time on this or string the calls over four or five days. Try to get your calls all made within two days. Take copious notes; outline your questions ahead of time and ask the same questions in each phone interview. Rank the responses from 1 to 10.

The most important task is to verify the skills and background presented on the resume. Ask for specific details about how they spend (or spent) their time at work, whether they have managed others, what kind of training they had. It is not unknown for employees to exaggerate or even lie on resumes. Dig out the real facts. Once you are satisfied, go on to other features of the resume, but do leave time to describe the employment opportunity you have.

Most hiring managers assume that candidates need the job you are offering. But don't make the mistake of assuming that candidates need it desperately. Perhaps the candidate is simply testing the water—she is perfectly happy with her current employer or is comfortable enough in retirement. Perhaps she is well qualified and has several options available to her, including multiple job offers. As a small business owner, you may have to be a strong salesperson, both on the phone and in person.

To sum up, in a good initial phone interview you will do the following:

- Identify yourself, your position, your company, and why you are calling.
- Give a realistic description of the position; don't sugarcoat the job.
- Ask prepared questions of all the candidates and rank these responses.
- Find out why the person wants the job. If currently employed, why the change?
- When is the candidate available? If currently employed, how much notice would be expected?
- Is the candidate willing to travel? To relocate?
- Ask the candidate about salary expectations—try to get some idea of whether they match your planned compensation.

▸ Is overtime or weekend work expected? Willing to work evenings? (Anyone who ever worked for a retailer knows that the job hours are not nine to five, Monday to Friday.)

▸ Conclude in one of three possible ways: set up a personal interview; offer to call back after you have spoken to all the candidates; or decline further interest.

Deciding not to pursue a particular candidate and saying so on the phone is difficult, but if done correctly, it reduces the time and effort in hiring and forces you to be disciplined and businesslike. No one wants to say, right over the phone, that the individual is not an acceptable candidate. A simple, standard, and straightforward response is the best and easiest way to proceed: "Thank you for your time. Although you are a talented individual, I feel that your background does not match our current needs. I will keep your resume on file for future reference, and I wish you good luck in finding employment suited to your background." The matter is brought to closure, and you can now focus on other candidates. If you decide to go forward with an interview, make sure you get an e-mail address and home and mobile phone numbers (although they should have been on the résumé).

The Interview

Should you decide to invite a candidate into the office to meet you and other staff members, help yourself by helping the candidate. Make sure everyone has plenty of time—at least 90 minutes, perhaps as long as two hours. Confirm time, place, who they will meet, and in what order. If other interviewers are involved, explain their role in the company. Common sense matters, such as call-back numbers in case the interview has to be changed, location of your business, some directions on how to get there by car or public transportation, and a general outline of what will be discussed, including salary and benefits. Confirm everything in writing.

A traditional interview assumes that you found candidates with the right credentials; now it is time to kick the tires to see how well these individuals might fit in. Ask why they are leaving their current job, if they have one; try to find out what they would like to be doing in five years. Ask why they sought this position; it is important to understand a candidate's motivation. Finally, ask the candidates to speak about themselves, what they do well and where they need improvement.

If you are satisfied, it is time to narrow down the salary range, benefits, and other important issues. You should not have a candidate that you cannot afford in for an interview. Knowledge of what the candidate expects in terms of salary should have been clarified during the phone interview.

If at all possible, have others interview the candidates as well, asking the same kinds of questions, though not about salary or benefits. Some companies use small group interviews, especially if the candidate is in for a second round of interviews. But make it a friendly and supportive group, no more than two or three people. Pace questions and ask them in order, with a more senior person as the moderator and lead interviewer.

Some organizations use audition interviews—actually asking candidates to do the work they say they can do, whether typing, fixing a computer, using a financial accounting software package, or planting shrubs. On rare occasions, stress interviews are conducted to see how candidates react to difficult or awkward situations. As a rule, though, these are not very helpful and often cause more harm than good.

Employment Verification

State laws differ with regard to what you can and cannot do as part of your hiring process. If you want to conduct a credit report because the candidate has direct access to cash, you may have to give formal notice and share the results of your search with the candidate. Many states have regulations to protect a person's privacy, and you just cannot trample on these rights. This is true for drug testing and criminal background checks as well. Get expert, legal help if your verification needs are complicated.

Verification of employment usually results in the basics: confirmation of the start and end dates, title or position, whether the individual is eligible for rehire, and not much more. Former employers are reluctant to give out much more, and local law may put other limits on the information they can offer. No one wants to get sued for providing confidential, misleading, or outright wrong information. They tend, therefore, to be very conservative. There are, however, times when you can get much more if you ask the right questions and listen carefully. It is important to understand the relationship of your candidate to the person you are talking to: Human Resources department personnel, boss, coworker? Then try open-ended questions such as these:

- Tell me about her greatest strengths as an employee?
- Would she be rehired?
- Are there any areas where she needs improvement?
- How were her technical skills? What was she really good at on the job?
- Was she a self-starter?
- Could she handle multiple assignments at one time?
- Was she a team player?

▸ Did she show leadership?

▸ Would you (if a boss) have promoted her in the near future?

Take careful notes, but also listen for hesitation, uncertainty, too much enthusiasm, doubt, or rambling. Don't hesitate to ask the same question again, perhaps in different words. Listen for consistency and reasonable affirmation of a person's qualities.

Check every reference given by a candidate, even if the first two or three are positive and have convinced you that this is your person. You never know what you will learn. If you do get some negative news, you must decide whether it is a deal breaker. Perhaps the applicant was often late for work; this may or may not be an issue in your organization. Many companies have dropped rigid requirements about everyone working standard hours.

What you cannot overlook, no matter how much you like a candidate, are hints of dishonesty, poor judgment, excessive absenteeism, quarreling or other public displays, or any hints that personal style or behavior will be disruptive to the team. Small businesses must have employees who play nicely in the sandbox. This is an absolute must. You also need people who are flexible in their job assignments and their working habits. As the company grows, jobs change with the growth, and you need people who will grow with the company.

Making the Offer

It is important not to close any doors with other candidates until you are absolutely sure that your number-one choice will accept your offer. Be reasonable to other candidates by staying in touch and keeping them informed of your process generally. When you speak to your number-one candidate, make sure everything is covered the first time:

    position offered
    job responsibilities
    direct reports
    vacation and sick leave policies
    salary or rate of pay
    agreed start date
    hours and days to be worked
    travel requirements
    benefits
    bonus, if any, and what it is based on
    probationary period, if any

As an employer, you ask for proof that the candidate is eligible to work in this country; you can now do this online. You need identification, such as a driver's license or a passport, copies of which become part of the employee's permanent personnel file. The candidate must also fill out an IRS I-9 form.

The offer must be put in writing, not just casual e-mail. Fax or mail the document to the candidate and ask that it be signed and returned to you. It is not uncommon for workers to ask for some time to consider an offer. Family and friends will be consulted, maybe even a coworker or a boss from a previous job. Salary will be a big part of the decision, and if you don't offer a candidate who is already employed a reasonable boost in pay (say 10 to 15 percent) the change may not be worth the risk.

It is not uncommon for candidates to ask to negotiate salary, vacation time, working hours, and other aspects. Don't let a few thousand in compensation stop you from hiring a high-quality candidate; if, on the other hand, the prospective employee's expectations are much higher than you really can afford, don't get carried away and agree to terms you will regret later. Even if you lose this candidate over money issues, though it is inconvenient now, there will be other qualified candidates in your salary range. It will just take more time.

If you approach the negotiations with a win-win view, you have a much better chance of not only hiring a high-quality candidate but also starting the working relationship off on a solid and positive footing. Hard-line negotiations, even if won, leave a bad taste with people that can linger for years and may affect overall performance. Sometimes you can win and still lose.

Other Issues

Hiring (and firing, for that matter) can be complicated, stressful, and expensive—especially if you hire poorly or in haste. As the business grows and the hiring process accelerates, you will have to come to grips with a variety of issues. When is it time to put together a salary administration plan so that you don't end up with older employees making substantially less than new hires? Perceived unfairness in salary administration can be a real problem, even causing critical staff to leave for greener pastures.

It is one thing to hire a person, another matter entirely to train and orient someone to your company. Who will do this training? If you need someone from the outside, will a vendor do it for free or little cost?

What about special situations, such as making reasonable accommodations for a candidate who is handicapped? What about hiring ex-military personnel or even people who are on active reserve? There are specific laws both encouraging this kind of practice and protecting special groups.

Do you require each new worker to sign a noncompete or non-disclosure agreement? There are always specific rules governing these decisions. In some states, a strict noncompete agreement may be illegal because it is interpreted as an unreasonable restriction on a worker to make a living. Get legal advice for either of these practices.

Do you plan to test employees for drug use? It is important that you know what can and cannot be done. A qualified testing organization will ensure that your practices comply with the law.

Firing

Firing an employee is one of the most unpleasant parts of being the boss. Sometimes, though, it is necessary and can be the best action for both the terminated employee and your business. There are even times when firing is an immediate necessity for the safety and security of the rest of your staff.

Termination typically takes two forms: termination for cause and termination for poor performance. Termination for cause is a serious, threatening situation. Violence, drugs, alcoholism, stealing, and viewing pornography are some causes for termination. The situation must be handled immediately. First make sure that the employee is not a threat to himself or others. If the person is drunk and threatening, call security or the police immediately. Remain calm, do not touch the person, force him out of the office, or threaten him in any way. Have others witness the situation, someone from Human Resources if you have such a department. Tell the person he is terminated, get all company property back, and escort the employee to his locker, desk, or work area to collect his belongings. Make arrangements for any pay that is due, preferably on the spot.

Termination for poor performance or for a lack of it should be a more drawn-out affair because the reasons for the termination need documentation, and most companies make an effort to salvage the situation through some kind of remediation or training. The key is to talk to the employee and her supervisor to find out what is going on and why.

At the first hint of a problem, document that you have a situation that is not working. Find out if the problem is one that some simple training would help; perhaps the person just does not understand her responsibilities or how to meet them. If the employee is violating company policies and procedures, make sure she has written instructions with a goal of two weeks to get up to company standards. Follow up in two weeks. Give regular feedback and guidance. Set goals and times for future meetings to check performance. Tell the employee that she is on notice that if her work does not improve she will be fired. You may find that you have an unmotivated or unhappy employee—perhaps dissatisfied by the pay or the quality of the work. In this case, remediation is not going to work, but quick action will help you and the rest of your team.

If the decision is made to terminate an employee, move on it. Don't stall or delay. With sufficient documentation in hand, schedule a meeting, preferably with a witness—an office manager or someone from Human Resources. Be brief, clear, and simple when telling someone that he is terminated. Be specific. Do not engage in a discussion or dialogue at this stage. It is possible that the employee may get mean, lash out, or otherwise act out. End the meeting, escort the employee to the work area to collect personal belongings, get back company equipment and keys, and get the person off the premises just as soon as possible.

It is best to fire someone at the end of the day; it is less disruptive. You should have the final check ready, including any severance. Even if the employee has been with you for a short time, some small severance is appropriate—at the very least paying two weeks' wages. For long-term employees, two weeks plus a week for every year of employment is common. If severance is offered, it should be given in exchange for a written statement that the employee will not sue the company for wrongful termination.

Most people in the workforce are hired on the basis of "employment at will," meaning that they are without benefit of a written contract and can be fired for good cause, bad cause, or no cause at all. The law mitigates this somewhat by imposing rules against firing someone because of obvious discrimination, and you cannot fire someone if the action violates state law. For example, you cannot fire an employee for filing for workman's compensation. Employees under some kinds of labor contracts cannot be fired without due process or specific compensation. Small businesses tend not to have labor contracts, so this is usually not an issue.

Once a staff member has been fired, it is important to communicate to other workers either by memo or, preferably, in person about what has happened. You don't have to go into great detail, and you can use the situation to emphasize the value and importance of every team member present.

Finally, make sure that passwords are changed and other security measures are taken, such as changing locks. If a fired employee comes back to your place of business, calls or threatens you, or promises to sue, call you lawyer and, if necessary, the police.

Because the act of firing someone is so traumatic, managers do most anything to rationalize an employee's work history so as to not take this step. Delaying the inevitable is a mistake. The sooner you act, the better off you and your company will be. Just remember: firing should be done with the same courtesy and respect that you used in hiring.

Resources

U.S. Department of Labor

The U.S. Department of Labor has an extensive website at which small employers can find a great deal of information about employment law and fair hiring: www.dol.gov/compliance/topics/hiring -issues.htm#overview.

Ask the Right Questions, Hire the Best People

For more on conducting proper and productive interviews, consider *Ask the Right Questions, Hire the Best People,* by Ron Fry (Career Press, 2010). In addition to being very readable, the book has a nice section on how to conduct phone interviews. But its main feature is a list of questions you should ask along with the kinds of answers you should expect from a qualified candidate.

EIGHT

Finance Basics

Things to know before starting a business:

- ▸ *You must become financially literate before starting a business.*
- ▸ *Financial management is every employee's business.*
- ▸ *Balance sheets, income statements, and statements of cash flow are company snapshots in time.*
- ▸ *Vertical and horizontal analyses are critical tools for judging financial progress of a company.*
- ▸ *Standard financial ratios help explain your business.*

Financial Literacy

There is a tendency, especially in small and home-based businesses, not to focus on financial basics and to delegate (or ignore completely) the fundamentals of good financial management. Needless to say, as a business owner or manager you are not necessarily going to become a specialist by mastering the concepts from books, seminars, or training courses. But you must be able to understand the financial dynamics of your business. Are matters improving or getting worse? Do you know the reasons for changes in the financial condition of your business? Is a particular department or individual manager performing as expected and as needed?

Business owners and managers need to be partners with their internal financial managers (if they have people on staff to assist in these functions) as well as external advisors such as accountant and tax preparer. The IRS does not accept ignorance of the facts as an excuse, and neither will your partners, investors, lenders, or other stakeholders.

New business owners need to understand (and use, for that matter) the tools of business. They need to be able to speak with confidence to outsiders, especially investors, lenders, and bankers. Simple questions about your financial condition can trip you up, make you appear amateurish or not quite sure about how really to operate the financial side of a business.

Many readers will recognize immediately that data has to be viewed in its proper context. For example, is yours a seasonal business—a commercial greenhouse, for example? If so, then samplings of financial performance in April or May will be entirely different than the same measures in December or January. Or, to take another example, sales patterns, cash flow, and marketing expenses for companies that are business-to-business (B2B) are entirely different from those for a consumer product company (business-to-consumer, B2C). It makes little sense to compare one to the other—the proverbial apples and oranges.

Seek out other companies like yours; get to know your competitors or groups that are similar (manufacturing or service). Join the industry association or at least the local or regional chapter. If you join your industry association, you can use the data they accumulate. (You may be terribly troubled that your receivables are typically well over 60 days from date of invoice; on investigation, you may find that the industry norm is even worse. It is all a matter of perspective.)

The basics of financial statements and measures of financial performance, with few exceptions, are related. It is important to understand that the data needed for some calculations of performance, which are available from the financial statements, may need to be refined. If you are looking for total costs of employment, for example, you can typically find this information on the income statement. However, if you need a subset of this figure (maybe loaded costs for support staff), you need to work with your financial officer or accountant to extrapolate that number.

Understanding how a balance sheet is constructed and what it communicates is important; the same is true for a profit-and-loss statement and a statement of cash flows. All are related and all are snapshots of your business each time they are prepared. Financial statements are your presentation pieces to investors, bankers, trade creditors— including your management team and employees. Your accountant or financial officer (with the approval and oversight of your outside auditor) prepares these statements quarterly and at year's end.

The Importance of Financial Statements

Financial statements are nothing more than tools to this ultimate end: Ensure that the company is fiscally sound and, as a result, can meet its stated goals and obligations. Financial statements are used in both profit and not-for-profit organizations. The former clearly has a responsibility to investors and owners (and other stakeholders

as well) to make a profit and build wealth. The latter do not specifically have profit as a primary goal, but they certainly do have a
secondary goal to be fiscally and financially responsible and thus
able to further their primary goal—educational, philanthropic,
professional, or social service.

Financial statements are nothing more than snapshots of a business at any given time—end of the month, quarter, or fiscal year.
They can only freeze time and look back; unlike budgets and sales
projections, which look forward, they cannot tell you how you will
or might do in the future. Their goal is to show how the company
did for the period being reviewed—did it make a profit, or not? Did
sales increase and were overhead and costs reasonable and under
control? As important, if not more so, financial statements allow
management, investors, bankers, vendors, and any stakeholders to
compare this period (month, quarter, or year) to previous periods—
in order to track progress.

Financial statements are just part of the toolkit managers use,
but they are probably the most important. For one thing, they allow
everyone to look back objectively and try to understand what went
right and what did not. They are a major component of the process
called financial management. Just how well are the assets of the
organization being used vis-à-vis the goals and objectives of the
organization? Many feel that financial statements are best used
as planning tools, as a means to correct the errors of the past and
improve future performance.

Everyone Is a Financial Manager

Almost every decision a supervisor, team leader, or a manager
makes—even the smallest ones—has a financial consequence. No
matter what department you are part of or your own educational

background, everyone needs to be and is a financial manager. Understand the essentials of financial management, and with experience you will come to appreciate that financial knowledge helps your overall decision making and team leadership skills. You learn to plan better and solve problems more efficiently because you understand the financial ramifications of your actions.

Finance can be the common language that links all members of an organization. The more you know, the better you are able to communicate and share your department's goals and objectives. With the other departments, you can analyze the victories of the past (as well as the defeats) and set a course for the future.

Further, entrepreneurs with backgrounds in marketing, advertising, human resources, planning, information technology, and customer service who know their numbers are highly attractive to investors and lenders. They can speak to the outside world with confidence, communicate plans for new products and services, discuss budgets and sales projections intelligently, and demonstrate that they are not only experts in their respective fields but skilled businesspeople in general.

Financial Statements Are Not Rocket Science ·····

Understanding and reading financial statements are not nearly as difficult as some make these tasks out to be. If you can follow a recipe or apply for a loan, you can learn how to read financial statements. Once you understand how they are organized (very efficiently) and once you understand the components of the various statements, you can go to any company's financial statements and understand their business. Remember: The basic role of financial statements is to show where the money is now, where it came from, and where it went.

There can be a variety of financial statements created in the course of a business, but three are primary:

Income statements show how much money a company made (or did not) and how much was spent over a period of time.

Balance sheets show what a company owns and what it owes at a fixed point in time.

Cash flow statements show the exchange of money between a company and the rest of the world over a period of time.

Income Statements

An income statement shows how much revenue a company earned over a specific period (usually a year or a quarter). An income statement also shows the costs and expenses associated with earning that revenue. It reflects the true cost of operating the business for the time indicated. The literal bottom line of the income statement shows the company's net earnings or losses, and thus how much the company earned or lost over the period.

To understand how income statements are set up, think of them as a set of stairs. Examine exhibit 8-1, the income statement for The Great Company for the year ending 2011. You start at the top with the total amount of sales made during the accounting period. For The Great Company in this period, gross sales amounted to $3,900,000. Then you go down, one step at a time. At each step, you make a deduction for certain costs or other operating expenses associated with earning the revenue. At the bottom of the stairs, after deducting all of the expenses, you learn how much the company actually earned or lost during the accounting period.

Revenue

At the top of the income statement is the total amount of money from sales of products or services. This top line is often referred to as *gross revenues* or *sales*. It is called *gross* because expenses have not been deducted from it yet. So the number is unrefined.

The next lines show money the company does not expect to collect on certain sales. This could be due, for example, to sales discounts or merchandise returns. When you subtract the returns, allowances, and discounts from the gross revenues, you arrive at the company's net revenue. In the case of The Great Company, the first set of deductions for adjustments to gross revenues amounts to $43,000. As a percentage of the gross sales, these adjustments are relatively minor, only 1.1 percent (43,000/3,900,000). This low number may indicate that The Great Company has very few problems with quality, hence low returns from customers or resellers. Or the company may be very conservative about discounts awarded over and above its stated selling prices; obviously, some exceptions were made, because they allowed extraordinary discounts in the amount of $23,000. Deducting these expenses from gross sales gives a net sales figure.

Moving down from the net revenue line, there are entries that represent various kinds of expenses. The line after net sales (revenues) typically shows the cost of goods sold, or the cost of sales. This number tells you the amount of money the company spent to produce the goods or services it sold during the accounting period.

Exhibit 8-1 shows that the company spent $1,230,000 on the cost of goods, almost 32 percent (1,230,000/3,900,000) of gross sales. The percentage is slightly higher if you use net sales instead of gross sales. Most observers would prefer the more conservative ratio, but the differences are quite small in this case. If instead this business had much larger returns, allowances, or discount

EXHIBIT 8-1 ▸ The Great Company: Year-End Income Statement, 2011

Revenue

Gross sales	$ 3,900,000		$3,900,000
Returns and allowances	($ 20,000)		
Discounts	($ 23,000)	($ 43,000)	
Net sales			$3,857,000
Cost of goods sold	($1,230,000)		
Gross profit			$2,627,000

Operating Expenses

Selling expenses			
Advertising	($ 46,000)		
Salaries	($ 325,000)		
Travel and entertainment	($ 33,000)		
Conventions	($ 29,900)		
Print and catalogs	($ 16,000)	($ 449,900)	
General and administrative expenses			
Officer salaries	($ 775,000)		
Employee salaries	($ 431,000)		
Depreciation	($ 1,200)		
Mortgage	($ 55,000)		
Supplies	($ 5,600)		
Shipping	($ 39,000)		
Equipment	($ 59,000)	($1,365,800)	
Operating Income			$ 811,300
Other expenses			
Interest expense	($ 225,000)		
Interest income	$ 0		
Other expenses net (taxes)	($ 136,000)	($ 361,000)	
Net Income			$ 450,300

experiences, net sales rather than gross should be used to determine the percentage of cost of goods sold to sales.

Subtracting the cost of goods sold from the net revenues, you arrive at a subtotal called *gross profit* or sometimes *gross margin*. In this case the income statement tells us that the gross profit was $2,627,000 (3,857,000 − 1,230,000). It is considered gross because there are certain expenses that have not yet been deducted. From an operating manager's point of view, this is where the rubber meets the road. The Great Company has done an excellent job generating sales, and the cost of goods sold seems reasonable—about one-third of net sales. It is the ability to control expenses that determines the success or failure of the business. (Remember, there are really only two ways to become profitable or increase profitability: above the line, you can increase sales; below this line, you can reduce expenses.)

Gross profit (gross margin) is often expressed as a simple percentage of net sales. In this case it is 69 percent, which is excellent by almost any industry standard. Because the cost of goods (or services) sold can vary so widely across industries, management has to examine the gross profit as a percentage of sales in light of what competing companies are doing—both locally and nationally and, increasingly, internationally. Although a gross profit of 69 percent may seem excellent, if competitors are getting even higher margins, then The Great Company is lagging behind. On the other hand, if industry standards are as low as 45 percent gross profit, The Great Company is a stellar company. And, again, what did this company do last year and the year before? Where is the trend going? If 69 percent is better than the past years, management can take a good deal of satisfaction in how it has managed the cost of goods sold and increased sales simultaneously.

Operating Expenses

The next section deals with selling expenses. These are expenses that go toward supporting a company's operations (direct selling and marketing efforts) for a given period, such as salaries for sales-people and travel costs. Marketing expenses are another example. Operating expenses are different from cost of goods sold, which were deducted above, because operating expenses cannot be linked directly to the production of the products or services being sold. These expenses are also discretionary; if business is poor, an entre-preneur can reduce advertising or marketing expenses.

For The Great Company in this period, the only real operating expenses identified are costs associated with sales and marketing, those incurred in some kind of customer contact or communi-cation. Essentially, the company has identified all the expenses that keep the sales and marketing teams in the field and in direct communication with the customer (e.g., catalogs and conven-tions). The $449,900 is a reasonable percentage of net sales (12 percent, 449,900/3,857,000) and of gross profit (17 percent, 449,900/2,627,000). In fact, on the basis of these figures someone could argue that, if management invested further in more catalogs, salespeople, and conventions, net sales might increase significantly.

Next comes general and administrative expenses. Generally, this is a rather large grouping of expenses that are related neither to the costs of goods sold nor to the operating (selling) effort. They include the nuts and bolts of most businesses: support personnel, senior management, new equipment, and rent or mortgage. This is the largest expense item on the income statement, 35 percent of net sales (1,365,800/3,857,000) and 52 percent of gross profit (1,365,800/2,627,000). As every team leader and operating man-ager knows, one of the easiest ways to increase profitability is to reduce these below-the-line expenses. Postponing decisions to buy new equipment or eliminating the so-called nonessential jobs has a dramatic effect on the bottom line. As with every company, the cost of employees (managers, officers, and administrative employees) is the greatest expense; this figures includes social security payments, retirement benefits, and health insurance. In this case the total cost is $1,531,000, over half of the gross profit for the year.

Depreciation is also deducted from gross profit. Depreciation takes into account the wear and tear on some assets, such as machinery, tools, and furniture, that are used over the long term. Companies spread the cost of these assets over the periods they are used, a process called *depreciation* or *amortization*. The charge for using these assets during the period is a fraction of the original cost of the assets.

Operating Income

After all operating expenses are deducted from gross profit, you arrive at operating income (profit before interest and income tax expenses). This is often called *income from operations*. This figure purposely excludes any income from investments, rentals (a company might lease out part of its offices or warehouse), or any other extraordinary cash flow such as sale of equipment.

When examining an income statement, investors and bankers want to see what generates the profits; if they find that the company is profitable, that is favorable. But if they find out from the income statement that the major source of the profit is not from operations (its main business) but from rental income, for example, that is not good. The business is not operating as its charter and business plan suggests. In the case of The Great Company, there is no extraordinary income, and thus the company is operating at full tilt in its market.

Next, companies must account for interest income and interest expense. *Interest income* is the money companies make from keeping their cash in interest-bearing savings accounts, money market funds, and the like. *Interest expense* is money companies pay in interest for money they borrow. Some income statements show interest income and interest expense separately. Some income statements combine the two numbers. The interest income and expense are then added or subtracted from the operating profits to arrive at operating profit before income tax.

Finally, income tax is deducted (shown as part of other expenses net), and you arrive at the bottom line: net income (profit) or net losses.

Net Income

Net income (or loss) tells you how much the company actually earned or lost during the accounting period. Did the company make a profit, or did it lose money? The example of The Great Company shows that it is a profitable organization, having generated revenues of $3,900,000, with a net income after interest and taxes of $450,300, or about 11.5 percent of total revenues (450,300/3,900,000). By most standards this would be a successful year. But it may or may not be as good as other companies in the same industry group. And it may or may not be as good as the company has done in previous years. In fact, it could indicate serious problems, even though there was profit.

Management is always looking at the trends—over three or four quarters or even three or four years. Where is the trend going, and what does it mean? Management, through various ratios and formulas, will take this income statement apart to see which expenses have increased (e.g., as a percentage) relative to either total revenue or gross profit, or both. In fact, the income statement can show literally dozens of important facts and trends about expenses and the types of expenses and how well management is using the assets at hand to create wealth for shareholders.

Many income statements for for-profit companies include a calculation of earnings per share (EPS). This calculation tells you how much money shareholders would receive for each share of stock they own if the company distributed all of its net income for the period. To calculate EPS, you take the total net income and divide it by the number of outstanding shares of the company.

In the example above, assume that there are 500 shares outstanding of The Great Company's common stock; preferred stock, if any, is not included in this calculation. Thus we know that in theory the company could pay shareholders $900.60 in the form of a dividend for each share of stock they hold.

The dividend policies adopted by management or the board of directors are extremely important. Companies that are new or growing rapidly rarely distribute dividends, since the cash represents (as retained earnings) the money that will be used to expand the company further, either by internal growth or through acquisition. These same retained earnings could also be used to pay down debt, thus reducing operating expenses in future years. Whether well established or brand new, companies almost never distribute all of their earnings to shareholders.

Balance Sheet

A balance sheet provides detailed information about a company's assets, liabilities, and shareholder equity. It is literally a balance or a scale: assets less liabilities must always equal the equity in the business. Exhibit 8-2 is a sample balance sheet for The Great Company for year 2011. For simplicity's sake, not every possible line item is shown on this balance sheet. Balance sheets for for-profit companies are different from those for not-for-profit companies; the latter do not have stockholders who own equity in the organization.

In not-for-profits, some other category is used to balance the equation—perhaps reserves or assets for continuing operations.

In our example, the balance sheet shows assets at the top, followed by liabilities, with shareholder's equity at the bottom. In another common balance sheet arrangement, the left side of the sheet lists company assets, and the right side lists liabilities and shareholder's equity.

Assets

Assets are generally listed based on how quickly they will be converted into cash, with current assets followed by noncurrent assets. Liabilities are generally listed based on their due dates. A balance sheet, then, shows a snapshot of a company's assets, liabilities, and shareholder equity at the end of the reporting period. It does not show the flows into and out of the accounts during the period.

For for-profit companies like The Great Company, shareholder equity is calculated as assets minus liabilities. Assets are the resources a company owns that have value; that is, if they were put on the market today, they would generate cash. This typically means that they can either be sold or used by the company to make products or provide services that can then be sold. Assets include physical property such as buildings, trucks, equipment, and materials used to make products and finished inventory. Not all assets are physical: databases, trademarks, and patents are intangibles that have value and can be sold. Of course, cash itself is an asset, as are the investments a company owns outside of its core business (stocks, bonds, mutual funds, certificates of deposits, and more). Even goodwill is an asset. Consider a fast-food company that has been advertising and marketing its products for years; the company name and the customers' positive experiences at its stores constitute substantial assets that can be valued for financial management purposes.

EXHIBIT 8-2 ▸ The Great Company: Year-End Balance Sheet, 2011

Assets

Current assets		
Cash	$ 334,000	
Accounts receivable	$ 698,000	
Short-term securities	$ 44,000	
Inventory	$ 650,000	
Total current assets		$1,726,000
Long-term investments	0	
Fixed assets		
Building (less accumulated depreciation)	$3,450,000	
Equipment (less accumulated depreciation)	$ 820,000	
Total fixed assets		$4,270,000
Intangible assets		
Patents (less accumulated depreciation)	$ 16,000	
Trademarks (less accumulated depreciation)	$ 56,000	
Customer lists	$ 89,000	$ 161,000
Deferred charges (prepaid expenses)		$ 26,500
Total assets		$6,183,500

Liabilities and Shareholder's Equity

Current liabilities		
Accounts payable	$1,240,000	
Bank line	$ 179,000	
Total current liabilities		$1,419,000
Noncurrent liabilities		
Notes payable	$1,670,000	
Mortgage	$2,517,500	
Total noncurrent liabilities		$4,187,500
Total liabilities		$5,606,500
Stockholder equity		
Capital stock	$ 45,000	
Paid-in capital	$ 250,000	
Retained earnings	$ 282,000	
Total stockholder equity		$ 577,000
Total liabilities and shareholder equity		$6,183,500

In the current business environment, it is not uncommon for intangible assets to be the major component of many balance sheets. Unlike tangible assets, these nonmonetary assets cannot be touched or physically measured in the usual sense, but they can represent the greatest portion of a company's value. Many of the world's largest economies have evolved beyond traditional agriculture, mining, transportation, or manufacturing; the current and future growth within these economies is based on services, financial and otherwise, including information storage, management, and retrieval. In our example, however, The Great Company is a traditional business; most of its assets are fixed in buildings and equipment.

There are two primary forms of intangibles: *legal intangibles*, such as trade secrets (formulas, databases, and customer records), copyrights, patents, trademarks, and goodwill, and *competitive intangibles,* such as operating systems, procedures, and productivity improvements.

Balance sheets typically break down assets into five groups: current assets, long-term investments, fixed assets, intangible assets, and deferred charges. This makes it easier, when you are analyzing a company's balance sheet, to understand the kinds of assets (hence value) and their liquidity (how quickly can they be converted to cash).

Current assets. For most companies, assets are considered current if they will be used up or converted to cash within one year. Examples of current assets are cash, securities you plan to sell within a year, accounts receivables, and inventory. The Great Company has current assets totaling $1,726,000, most of which is in accounts receivables and inventory. The company has invested an additional $44,000 in short-term securities; this can typically be viewed as an emergency fund to help in times when cash and collection of receivables are lagging.

Long-term investments. As opposed to short-term assets, these are investments that you plan to hold for more than one year before liquidating. The most common examples of long-term investments are stocks or bonds or other financial instruments. The Great Company shows no long-term investments. You can assume that this is a fairly new or smaller company; its assets are used for its core business, and none have been diverted for longer-term securities. As the company matures, long-term investments may be a good strategy, but generally managers and owners want to use assets to build the core business, not invest or speculate long-term.

Fixed assets. Property, plant, trucks, computers, office furniture, and equipment are some of the most common types of fixed assets. Thus, they are physical assets (as opposed to intangible assets). They are not held for sale or liquidation but are used for the normal course of business.

As the old saying goes, the minute you buy and drive a new car out of the showroom, it becomes a used car. Like the car, all fixed assets deteriorate. One of the easiest to understand is a new computer system. You know that because of the rapid changes in technology and systems, the minute a new computer system is installed it is on the way to being out of date. Thus, fixed assets are depreciated. In the case of The Great Company, the value of the building and equipment in the fixed asset category is figured minus depreciation.

Intangible assets. As discussed above, intangible assets have a long-term life and are not physical. For example, a franchise license, patents, and the rights to this book are intangible assets. If The Great Company were in the software development business, publishing, or movie production, its assets in the intangible category would be substantially higher. Again, note that patents and trademarks are evaluated less accumulated depreciation. These assets deteriorate over time, just like fixed assets. One could even make the case that the third intangible asset on this balance sheet, customer lists, should also be depreciated; the financial managers of The Great Company, however, have determined that active list management and list building by the marketing department keep these lists current and valuable, so no deterioration of this asset is recorded.

Deferred charges (prepaid expenses). These kinds of charges represent expenditures or money paid out that has already been incurred, has been recorded on the balance sheet as an asset, but is expected to become an expense over time or through the normal course of business. Thus, deferred expenses are sometimes called *prepaid expenses.* Office supplies, prepaid rentals, and prepaid insurance are examples of deferred charges. The Great Company shows little prepaid expense: $26,500, or less than one-half of 1 percent of total assets.

Liabilities

Liabilities are amounts of money a company owes to others. They can include all kinds of obligations: money borrowed from a bank to launch a new product; rent for use of a building; money owed to suppliers for materials; payroll a company owes to its employees; environmental cleanup costs; and taxes owed to the government. Liabilities also include obligations to provide goods or services to customers in the future. There are both current and noncurrent (long-term) liabilities.

Current liabilities. Current liabilities are those due within one year and are paid out of current assets, typically cash on hand. Health insurance, money owed to suppliers, and monthly payroll are examples of current liabilities. For our example of The Great Company (for simplicity's sake), accounts payable represents a large portion of current liabilities: salaries, insurance, inventory, utilities, and items used in the normal course of running a business. The bank line (as opposed to notes payable farther below) is a short-term credit function that helps the company meet everyday obligations. The company borrows and pays back on this line as per the agreement with the lender. In theory, it too would be paid off in one year, although customary practice is to renew the line yearly and roll over any balance into next year's line.

Noncurrent liabilities. Noncurrent liabilities are those that are expected to be paid over an extended period of time. Examples of noncurrent liabilities include a bank loan due in five years and bonds with a maturity of more than one year underwritten to finance the operations of a company. In the case of The Great Company, there is a long-term bank loan that was used for start-up and initial inventory; the largest long-term obligation is that of the mortgage on the building. Rather than be a renter, management felt that buying the building in which the company is located would be prudent; thus the mortgage is the largest obligation, short- or long-term, that the company has.

Shareholder equity. Shareholder equity is sometimes called *capital* or *net worth.* If the company were to be sold today (or if it went out of business and the assets of the company were liquidated), this would be the money left after all the other bills and obligations, short- and long-term, were paid. It also represents the net proceeds of selling off all the assets of the company. This remaining money belongs to the shareholders, the owners of the company. Shareholders become shareholders because they expect that, if or when the company is liquidated, shareholder equity is greater than the investment capital used to start the company; ideally, the net worth will be large enough to justify the financial commitment made to this company in the first place. In other words, if the money had been invested in a conservative financial instrument instead of the company, would the shareholders be better off now?

The Great Company balance sheet shows initial paid-in capital of $250,000 (that, with the long-term debt, was the funding used to start the company). Retained earnings are monies earned but reinvested in The Great Company to fund operations and expand the business. Depending on management's expectations of need, some of the earnings each year may be paid out as dividends to the shareholders. Typically, in a newer or smaller company, dividends are not paid, for most of the retained earnings are needed to build the company and acquire further assets.

Cash Flow Statements

Cash flow statements report a company's inflow and outflow of cash. The monitoring of cash flow is important because a company needs enough cash on hand to pay its expenses and purchase assets at any given time. Whereas an income statement can tell you whether a company made a profit, a cash flow statement can tell you whether the company generated cash. A cash flow statement shows changes over time rather than absolute dollar amounts at a point in time. It uses and reorders the information from a company's balance sheet and income statement.

The bottom line of the cash flow statement shows the net increase or decrease in cash for the period. Generally, cash flow statements are divided into three main parts. Each part reviews the cash flow from one of three types of activities: operating activities, investing activities, and financing activities. Exhibit 8-3 shows cash flow for The Great Company. Generally, the larger the operation, the more complicated the statement of cash flow. Established companies have a variety of sources and uses of cash, which may not ever be utilized in a small or emerging business.

Cash Flow from Operations

The first part of a cash flow statement analyzes a company's cash flow from net income or losses. For most companies, this section of the cash flow statement reconciles the net income (as shown on the income statement) with the actual cash the company received from or used in its operating activities. To do this, it adjusts net income for any noncash items (such as adding back depreciation expenses) and adjusts for any cash that was used or provided by other operating assets and liabilities.

The Great Company shows a net income $450,300, and this is reflected as net income on the cash flow statement. Management added back depreciation taken, for a total net cash flow from operations of $502,300 (450,300 + 52,000). The greater the amount of cash generated from operations, the less a company has to depend on income from investments or from the capital markets (i.e., cash flow from financing).

Cash Flow from Investments

The second part of a cash flow statement shows the cash flow from all investing activities, which generally include purchases or sales of long-term assets, such as property, plant, and equipment, as well as investment securities. If a company buys a piece of machinery, the cash flow statement reflects this activity as a cash outflow from investing activities because it used cash. If the company sells off some investments from an investment portfolio, the proceeds from the sales show up as a cash inflow from investing activities because they provided cash.

EXHIBIT 8-3 ▸ **THE GREAT COMPANY:**
YEAR-END STATEMENT OF CASH FLOW, 2011

Cash Flow from Operations

Net income	$ 450,300	
Adjustments		
Depreciation	$ 52,000	
Net cash flow from operations		$ 502,300

Cash Flow from Investments

Purchase of equipment	($ 125,000)	
Purchase of computer system	($ 277,700)	
Sales of used equipment	$ 16,000	
Net cash flow from investments		($386,700)

Cash Flow from Financing

Issuance of common stock	$ 0	
Long-term debt	$1,000,000	
Short-term bank loan	($ 225,000)	
Mortgage payment on building	($ 55,000)	
Loan payment to officer	($ 156,000)	
Net cash flow from financing		$ 564,000
Net Increase (Decrease) in Cash		$ 679,600

The only positive cash flow for The Great Company in this group is from the sale of some used equipment, a minor item. The company has not reached the stage where it can expect to generate substantial cash flow from investments, whether short- or long-term. This section of the cash flow statement does, however, indicate that the company continues to invest in its core business by purchasing new equipment and a new computer system.

Cash Flow from Financing

The third part of a cash flow statement shows the cash flow from all financing activities. Typical sources of cash flow include cash raised by selling stocks and bonds and by borrowing from banks. Likewise, paying back a bank loan shows up as a use of cash.

The Great Company in year 2011 did borrow additional funds on a long-term basis, and this is reflected in the cash flows from financing activities. Everything else indicates cash outlays to repay debt and pay down the mortgage for the company premises.

In the end, The Great Company shows an increase in cash of $679,600, which will be used on a forward basis to fund operations and pay down debt—along with additional cash flow from operations and other sources in the next fiscal year.

Analyzing Financial Statements

It is common practice to do some analysis of the core financial statements companies produce quarterly and annually. There are a good number of interested parties, whether a company is large or small, privately held or owned by shareholders—whether its shares are traded on an exchange or not. In general, the interested parties are looking for answers to essentially the same questions, although a banker may have particular interests that a shareholder is not nearly as concerned about. Essentially, all stakeholders have these common concerns:

How is the business doing?

Is it profitable or not?

What strengths does the company have?

What are the weaknesses?

How does it compare to its competitors?

Is the business improving, or is it in slow (or rapid) decline?

Various standard tools are used in the analysis of financial statements, usually the balance sheet and income statement. This is often called "spreading the sheets," a quaint phrase to describe the process of looking in depth at what is going on and why.

A variety of quantitative tools are used for this purpose. Many stakeholders are concerned about specific issues, owner/managers have one set of concerns from an operating point of view, and lenders (your friendly bank) and investors may have different perspectives. There are simple ratios and formulas to help each group. Creditors of all stripes, banks as well as vendors (credit sales of inventory, services, and supplies to your company), are interested in your ability not just to repay the credit granted but to pay it on time.

Investors focus on the current and future viability of the company and whether investing in this company makes sense vis-à-vis other available investment opportunities. They tend to balance risk and reward and are concerned about the current and future earnings of the company. Management, of course, is interested in all of these issues, since it has full responsibility (and often, ownership) of the enterprise. It is essentially its job to manage for profitability and sustainability for the benefit of all parties—owners, employees, lenders, and suppliers.

Key managers in accounting, human resources, sales and marketing, production, and operations also need and want a variety of measures and tools to look more closely at specific activities within their departments and the effects of these activities on the total operation of the company.

There are two broad types of analysis—horizontal and vertical. A comparison of two or more years of financial information as reported by a company is *horizontal analysis*—literally going across the board from one year to the next and looking for significant changes in trends (both in dollars and as percentages). As you can readily understand, reporting just dollars may be deceptive. In *vertical analysis* the various sections of a financial statement are broken down by percentages for comparative purposes, either for a given reporting period or in combination with a horizontal analysis.

Horizontal Analysis

We can again use The Great Company statements to illustrate how horizontal analysis is used to spot problems and opportunities. For this illustration, we start with the area above the line (sales to gross profit) from the 2011 income statement (exhibit 8-1) and add the 2012 report for the same line items, as shown in exhibit 8-4.

First, compare gross sales; year 2012 saw a substantial increase in sales over year 2011: $700,000 (4,600,000 − 3,900,000). This is almost an 18 percent increase in sales. But there is a problem—not from gross sales or from the adjustments, which went up slightly, $2,000, from $43,000 to $45,000.

Focus on cost of goods sold. In year 2011 it was $1,230,000, and in year 2012 $1,844,000. In the first year the cost of goods sold is 32 percent of net sales; in the next reporting period it has risen to slightly over 40 percent of net sales. The result is that in the second year gross profit increased only $84,000 (2,711,000 − 2,627,000). The gross profit as a percentage of gross sales in 2011 is 67 percent (2,627,000/3,900,000); in the second year, gross profit as a percentage of gross sales decreases to 59 percent (2,711,000/4,600,000).

The first impression of The Great Company's 2012 year may have been positive, since revenues and gross profit were up in dollar terms. But as a percentage both were down, and cost of goods

EXHIBIT 8-4 ▸ **The Great Company: Horizontal Income Analysis**

	Income Statement 2011	Income Statement 2012
Revenue		
Gross sales	$3,900,000	$4,600,000
Returns and allowances	($ 43,000)	($ 45,000)
Discounts	($ 0)	($ 0)
Net sales	$3,857,000	$4,555,000
Cost of Goods Sold	($1,230,000)	($1,844,000)
Gross Profit	$2,627,000	$2,711,000

sold went up substantially. Investors and others looking at year 2012 would have expected the increase in gross sales (considering that discounts and allowances changed very little) to lead to a substantial increase in gross profit. Something is wrong with the cost of goods sold—perhaps the wrong vendors or a lack of attention to real costs. Or perhaps pricing did not keep up with inflation or the cost of goods; management may have tried to hold the line on prices in order to gain market share. No matter what management's rationale, the point is that horizontal analysis is absolutely crucial when looking at financial statements and the trends of a particular business.

Vertical Analysis

Vertical analysis is the use of a simple presentation strategy called *common-size statements*. It shows each item as a percentage;

typically a single important item, perhaps total assets on the balance sheet, is used as a base value, and everything else on the sheet is shown as a percentage of that base value. This information then, can be used in a horizontal analysis. For example, using the balance sheets from The Great Company for years 2011 and 2012 (exhibit 8-5), we can express the asset portion of the balance sheet in terms of percentages. By expressing various assets as a percentage of total assets, it is easy to spot any significant changes from one period to the next. This common-size format would easily show if current assets are decreasing and noncurrent assets are a higher percentage of total assets.

In this case, total assets have increased by $62,500 from one year to the next (6,246,000 − 6,183,500). Generally this is a good indicator that a company is building a strong asset base to fuel future growth and profitability. On the other hand, it is important to look at the kinds of assets that are increasing and what they may mean to the overall picture. This makes the case for using a base value to evaluate all assets on the balance sheet.

In this example, cash is decreasing as a percentage of total assets (5.4 percent in 2011 versus 3.98 percent in 2012), and accounts receivable is increasing as a percentage of the total (11.2 percent in 2011 versus 14 percent in 2012). This might indicate that customers are not paying or are not paying on time, which is a critical factor in the management of the firm. Even more important, current assets not only are less ($1,726,000 versus $1,684,000, down $42,000 in 2012), but the difference of current assets as a percentage of total assets is also an indication of a trend: In year 2011 current assets were 27.9 percent of total assets. In year 2012 they were 26.9 percent of total assets. Short-term liquidity (current assets) is extremely important for any company, particularly one in its formative years. Because liquidity is so important, lenders, vendors, and management itself would see that this situation needs immediate, corrective action.

EXHIBIT 8-5 ▸ The Great Company Balance Sheets: A Basis for Vertical Analysis

	Balance Sheet Year 2011		Balance Sheet Year 2012	
Current Assets				
Cash	$ 334,000		$ 249,000	
Accounts receivable	$ 698,000		$ 709,000	
Short-term securities	$ 44,000		$ 46,000	
Inventory	$ 650,000		$ 680,000	
Total current assets		$1,726,000		$1,684,000
Fixed Assets				
Building (less accumulated depreciation)	$3,450,000		$3,490,000	
Equipment (less accumulated depreciation)	$ 820,000		$ 890,000	
Total fixed assets		$4,270,000		$4,380,000
Intangible Assets				
Patents (less accumulated depreciation)	$ 16,000		$ 11,000	
Trademarks (less accumulated depreciation)	$ 56,000		$ 51,000	
Customer lists	$ 89,000	$ 161,000	$ 90,000	$ 152,000
Deferred Charge (Prepaid Expenses)		$ 26,500		$ 30,000
Total Assets		$6,183,500		$6,246,000

The Ultimate Goal

These basic examples of horizontal and vertical analysis lead us to the ultimate goal of any company: proper and sustainable cash management. Of the ratios and formulas in this book, the most important deal directly with cash flow and the sources and uses of cash and other assets.

Cash is and must be king. The ultimate goal of management is a cash management program that ensures proper liquidity—the right amount of cash available at the right time to meet your company's needs and objectives. With an effective cash management program, your company will neither be surprised by a developing cash shortage nor find itself with excess cash that should be put to work toward increasing sales and profitability.

Oddly, there are times when a negative cash flow is not necessarily bad—if it is planned as an opportunity cost directed to yielding greater benefits in a foreseeable period. A cash surplus, conversely, can cause your company almost as many problems as a deficit, even though they are less dire. A cash surplus represents assets that are making no direct contribution to your basic business. Even if these assets are invested wisely in financial investments, the yield may fall short of your company's return on investment. Yet there is little that can be done with short-term cash surpluses except to seek out the best possible yields for them. Unfortunately for most entrepreneurs, surplus cash is rare; the opposite is often the case.

The problem of imbalances notwithstanding, cash flow is manageable in most respects. You need not accept periodic cash emergencies as inevitable merely because they are common to your industry or have cropped up regularly in the past. There are any number of steps you can take to alleviate cash flow problems, surplus or deficit, or even eliminate them altogether.

You must keep two basic principles in mind: Cash should not flow into and out of your firm indiscriminately; and getting a handle on your cash flow situation must involve not only a subtraction of payables from receivables but a plan for dealing with the time lag between the two.

The easiest way to raise or lower your cash flow is to change the tactical pattern in which cash normally flows into and out of your firm over relatively short periods of time, say, four to six months. You can speed up collections or delay cash outflows to ease a cash deficit. Keep in mind, however, that changes in timing merely alter cash flow patterns for limited periods without changing the amount. They should have no impact on the future performance of the firm or on the firm's long-term investment, marketing, and growth goals.

Changes in policy for the sake of handling cash flow imbalances have much longer-term effects than timing changes. Such changes involve a commitment to alter previously planned objectives— in costs of operations, organization or replacement of plant and equipment, marketing and sales and investment in new products, or enhancing the customer service department.

From an operational point of view, such policy decisions could include raising or lowering inventory levels or spending on research and development. From a financial standpoint, you could decide to change your policy on dividends or capital investment programs. Of the two, dividend policy is the more flexible.

Resources

Suite101.com

Suite101.com is a rich website with a good deal of high-quality information—about not only financial management but all

aspects of business and entrepreneurship: www.suite101.com/
entrepreneurs.

Small Business Notes

Small Business Notes is another website worth reviewing. It offers
links to a variety of articles covering most of the important topics related to financial management and entrepreneurship: www
.smallbusinessnotes.com/operating/finmgmt.html.

Business Ratios and Formulas: A Comprehensive Guide

A well-researched book on ratios and formulas is *Business Ratios
and Formulas: A Comprehensive Guide* (Wiley, 2006), by Steven
M. Bragg. It has received high praise from readers and will serve
as a ready-reference throughout your business career. This is the
kind of book that will change little and should be kept on the shelf
(or your e-book reader) for future reference.

NINE

Cash Flow, Billing, and Collection Basics

Things to know before starting a business:

- ▸ *Paper profits are not cash.*
- ▸ *A business can be "profitable" on paper but still fail.*
- ▸ *Financial statements tell the past; financial projections predict the future.*
- ▸ *Predicting cash flow is essential; it tells you what you can spend and when.*
- ▸ *Good credit management is the key to predicting cash flow.*
- ▸ *Virtually every new business has cash flow problems, but there are ways to deal with them.*

Cash Is King

No matter the size of your company or the number of years you have (or have not) been in business, survival and prosperity are based on cash flow. So cash is truly king. In hard times cash has to be horded—expenditures slashed, personnel costs reduced, marketing downsized, and inventory kept lean. You simply cannot afford to make a mistake. When times are good, you can spend money to expand the business, perhaps buy out a competitor, add new products, and increase marketing and advertising. Your business strategy is in direct proportion to your cash flow.

There is a mistaken belief that being profitable is the most important aspect of a business. You may be profitable on paper (your income statement says you made money), but without the cash to back this up you will be out of business. Many young businesses make the mistake of trying to grow too fast—with the hope of getting the attention of investors and angels for financial backing. That strategy assumes that if you can demonstrate a strong growth pattern your business is viable.

In reality, though, for most small businesses it is not growth but cash flow and cash management that are so important. Be in the habit of following two golden rules:

- ▸ Never pay before you have to.
- ▸ Collect your money as soon as possible and before you spend.

The Importance of Good Working Capital Management

As every entrepreneur comes to know, effective working capital management constitutes one of the senior obligations of management—ensuring that the organization's cash assets are properly maintained and managed. Associated with this is an opportunity cost to the shareholders and the company; money invested in one area may cost opportunities for investment in other potentially more profitable areas. For example, if a department is operating with more working capital than is necessary, this overinvestment represents an unnecessary cost to the company—and this is just as true for the company as a whole if waste and inefficiency are present throughout the organization.

The objective of working capital management is to maintain the optimum balance of each of the working capital components. This includes making sure that funds are held as cash in bank deposits for as long as and in the largest amounts possible, thereby maximizing the interest earned. Nevertheless, depending on circumstances, there may be justification to move cash out much more quickly (especially if you anticipate new cash coming into the business from various sources regularly and predictably); such cash may more appropriately be invested in other assets—after all, that is why you are in business, not to earn interest on your money but to build and expand your base. Also, there can be substantial justification for using idle cash to reduce debt and other liabilities. The end result is cyclical: the more debt you reduce, the more cash you free up to reinvest in the business, the better you are able to generate more cash from operations.

Working capital management takes place on two levels:

▶ Ratio analysis can be used to monitor overall trends in working capital and to identify areas requiring closer management.
▶ The individual components of working capital can be effectively managed by using various techniques and strategies.

When considering these techniques and strategies, small business owners need to recognize that each department has a unique mix of working capital components. The emphasis that needs to be placed on each component varies according to department. For example, some departments have significant inventory levels; others have little if any inventory in their cash cycle.

Furthermore, working capital management is not an end in itself. It is an integral part of the company's overall management. The needs of efficient working capital management must be considered in relation to other aspects of the company's financial and nonfinancial performance.

Financial ratio analysis calculates and compares various ratios of amounts and balances taken from the financial statements. The main purposes of working capital ratio analysis are to indicate working capital management performance and to assist in identifying areas requiring closer management.

Three key points need to be taken into account when analyzing financial ratios:

▸ The results are based on highly distilled information. Consequently, situations that require control may not be apparent, and situations that do not warrant significant effort may be unnecessarily highlighted.
▸ Different companies face very different situations. Comparisons between them, or with global ideal ratio values, can be misleading.
▸ Ratio analysis is somewhat one-sided; favorable results mean little, whereas unfavorable results are usually significant.

Net Working Capital

The term *working capital* refers to the amount of capital that is readily available to an organization. Working capital is the difference between resources in cash or readily convertible into cash (current assets) and a company's commitments for which cash will soon be required (current liabilities). *Current assets* are resources that are in cash or will soon be converted into cash in the ordinary course of business. *Current liabilities* are commitments that will soon require cash settlement in the ordinary course of business. The formula is as follows:

Net working capital = Current assets – Current liabilities

In a company's balance sheet, these components of working capital are reported under the following headings:

CURRENT ASSETS

> cash and bank deposits (liquid assets)
> inventory (because it is assumed that it could be sold
>   quickly)
> accounts receivables
> short-term securities

CURRENT LIABILITIES

> bank line
> accounts payables
> other short-term liabilities

Take another look at exhibit 8-2, the balance sheet for The Great Company. The calculation of net working capital is as follows: total current assets are $1,726,000, and total current liabilities are $1,419,000, which means that the company has a net working capital of $307,000 as of year-end 2011. Total assets are greater than total liabilities, but there is clearly a problem. The company has invested most if its spare cash in fixed assets (building and equipment), which puts pressure on management to maintain sufficient current assets to cover current liabilities. The net working capital is a relatively small percentage of total liabilities: 17.7 percent (307,000/1,726,000). Management's major task, at this stage, based on the net working capital formula, is to concentrate on building cash to reduce liabilities before further company expansion.

Cash Flow Budget

Even the smallest company can and should use a cash flow budget. It is a simple document to make on a spreadsheet, and it is an essential tool for understanding what is going on in your business. In essence, you need two pieces of information before you can come to grips with cash management problems. You must find out just how much cash will flow into and out of your firm, and you should have an idea of when those inflows and outflows will occur.

The cash flow budget is used primarily to spotlight periods of too little or too much cash rather than for continuous control. (Rarely do smaller businesses have too much cash.) One important part of this exercise is to recognize periods when cash is going to be low long before you are confronted with the problem. You then have the time to obtain extra funds or to reduce spending in anticipation of a dry spell.

The cash flow budget content is taken primarily from your expense planning for the year. At some point you no doubt put together a basic profit-and-loss statement, indicating what would be spent for production, salaries, overhead, marketing, and so forth. What you may not have done is prepare this in such a way as to indicate when you would spend and how much money would come into the business from sales, borrowing, investors, and so forth.

To do this, you begin with the starting cash balance from the previous year. Exhibit 9-1 shows a cash flow budget for The Great Company. For the sake of discussion, assume that this is a cyclical business: more inventory is needed in the beginning of the year, more selling expenses are posted at the beginning of the year, and there is less of both at the end of the year. One thing remains constant: administration.

As you can easily see, for this company cash flow is a serious issue. The cash balances at the end of each quarter are meager, and something has to be done about that. This is a perfect illustration of why this exercise needs to be done, and regularly. One slip in cash collected, and the company will have to rely more and more on its bank line of credit—which has its limits. No bank will continue to lend if it sees cash flow going down, not up.

The owner can use this tool to explain to managers and employees alike why collecting cash sooner and spending it later are so important. In the example, management paid back some of the line of credit; had it fully understood its cash position, it might have not paid back the $10,000 and instead kept it for operating reserves. Not much interest will be saved, for the company will probably have to borrow it right back to pay for the heavy investment in production and marketing the next quarter (beginning of the fiscal year).

In fact, this cash flow budget suggests strongly that cost cutting is in order. Administration is the first category to look at to see what

EXHIBIT 9-1 ▸ **The Great Company:
Cash Flow Budget for (in 000s)**

	Q1	Q2	Q3	Q4	Rounded Average
Starting Cash	51	5	19	3	20
Cash collected	421	390	380	344	384
Total available cash	472	395	399	347	403
Cash Payments					
Sales/marketing	(100)	(90)	(85)	(30)	(76)
Administration	(138)	(138)	(138)	(138)	(138)
Production	(220)	(125)	(140)	(150)	(159)
Interest expense	(19)	(23)	(23)	(23)	(22)
Tax payments					
Dividends					
Loan payments				(10)	(5)
Sources of Cash					
Borrowing	50			10	10
Investors					
Ending Cash Balance	5	19	3	6	8

can be saved. Leaner inventory and reductions in spending for sales and marketing should follow. This situation will not turn around by itself, and if there are any unforeseen problems—such as a loss of a big customer or a slower economy in general—the company has no reserves to fall back on. The goal might be to increase end-of-quarter cash reserves by $10,000 each quarter so that at the start of the next fiscal year the company has something in the range of $50,000 cash balance.

The longer you are in business, the more reliable a cash flow budget becomes. Over three or four years you can find patterns to your business and then act on them by either reducing costs or using reserves. Borrowing should be used to build a business, not operate it once built. Besides, borrowing is both expensive and unreliable. You often cannot borrow when you need it the most.

Receipts and Disbursements Analysis

Receipts and disbursements analysis is the most common method of measuring cash flow. Because it is based on data recorded in the receipts and disbursements log—a basic bookkeeping ledger common to virtually all firms—the information itself is easy to obtain and organize no matter what kind of accounting software package you use. Most companies have relatively few general headings for their receipts and payments.

Receipts. There are only a limited number of ways for the average company to obtain cash. It is important, however, that each of them be differentiated in the receipt section of your analysis. Only if each category is identified can you properly monitor your cash receipts, as shown by the following:

▶ Collections are funds received from your accounts receivable. Normally, this represents the bulk of your cash inflow.
▶ Cash sales, or sales not involving credit, is usually the next largest category, but it stands far below collections in most companies. The exception, of

course, is if you own and operate a retail business, in which cash sales would greatly exceed collections from accounts receivable. For this discussion, cash sales includes credit card sales, for they are the same as cash—although it takes a day for the funds to be available in your account, and there is a bank fee that reduces the amount received.

▸ Nonoperating income. Few new companies routinely take in income from sources not necessarily associated with their primary business. This type of income includes dividend or interest income from investments, rental or lease income, royalties, and so forth.

▸ Special, nonrecurrent sources of income. The most common items in this category are new financings, such as equity investors in the business and disposal of surplus fixed assets. Income from any unusual source, though, could be included in this category. Again, small businesses rarely have income from the disposal of assets.

Disbursements. There are several payment categories that a firm can choose to identify in its analysis of cash flow. Here are some common headings:

▸ Supplier payments usually heads the list and can consist of cash payments as well as a reduction in accounts payable.

▸ Wages and salaries are difficult to control over the short term but can be managed over time.

- ▸ Overhead items such as heat, power, telephone, other utilities, and property taxes or rent are generally fixed and beyond management's control. Thus, you can usually bring these items together in one category.
- ▸ Income taxes can change rapidly and should be classified separately.
- ▸ Recurrent payments, such as interest on long-term bonds or dividend payments, should be grouped together under a separate heading.
- ▸ Irregular or special financial obligations, such as short-term loan repayments or special dividends, also should be in a separate category.
- ▸ Capital expenditures can sometimes be significant and sometimes amount to no more than a nominal influence on your cash payments. Nevertheless, they should be classified separately whenever possible.
- ▸ A special miscellaneous category should be included for extraordinary items (e.g., settlement of a lawsuit) or any other significant, nonrecurring item.

It is easy to prepare a receipts and disbursements planner to help you understand both how much and when cash moves in and out of the business under each of these categories. A simple spreadsheet document could look like exhibit 9-2. (For the sake of brevity, not all of the categories are included.)

To the seat-of-the-pants entrepreneur, this kind of planning may seem excessive and more trouble than it is worth. Remember, a lot depends on the size and complexity of your business. If you are working part-time from home and have just a few accounts or sources of income, a receipts and disbursements planner may be over the top. If, on the other hand, you have an active business in

EXHIBIT 9-2 ▸ **Receipts and Disbursements Planner**

	Q1	Q2	Q3	Q4	Total
Receipts					
Collections					
Cash					
Other					
Total receipts					
Disbursements					
Suppliers					
Wages					
Overhead					
Recurring					
Other					
Total disbursements					
Current Surplus (Deficit)					
Cash Balance: Beginning of Period					
Cash Balance: End of Period					

which you are engaged full-time, this is an essential tool for making your business successful. You must know the sources and uses of cash and when these activities will take place.

Preparing a Short-Term Cash Flow Forecast ·········

There are other basic tools new business owners might find useful, including the short-term cash flow forecast—which is designed to predict your company's cash flow for periods of up to a year. In its final form, a forecast looks much like a receipts and disbursements analysis. As with that process, the amount of detail you include in a forecast is up to you and largely depends on your industry and your own information requirements. Under most conditions, however, a relatively short list of headings suffices. Cover those items over which you have some control. If your rent is fixed, it would not be included; promotion money is variable and would be included.

The best way to prepare short-term cash forecasts is on a rolling monthly basis: the first forecast of the year covers January to December; the next, February to the following January; the next, March through the following February; and so on. In that way, you receive the earliest possible warning of a cash emergency.

The first step in preparing your forecast is to take a close look at your cash flow performance for the recent past. A review of the past several months can be most helpful in providing information on such items as inventory levels and accounts-receivable performance.

Next, make some broad assumptions about what your business will be like for the next year. Is it likely to be a good year, a mediocre year, or a bad one? Will costs rise at a faster rate than sales, or vice versa? Don't worry if you end up being wrong. Many times your assumptions will be wrong and your forecast will suffer as a result. On the other hand, you can always change the assumptions halfway through the year as you see how business is. By changing your assumptions, you will also adjust your cash flow forecast to reflect the new realities.

Here are some sample assumptions to make this process more concrete: sales will be the same as last year; receivables will be slower because we have more new customers and they tend to be slower than our traditional customers; the sales team needs new computers, and the inventory software must be upgraded.

The actual forecasting document looks much the same as the receipts and disbursement analysis planner shown in exhibit 9-2. Rather that setting this up on a quarterly basis, this document would be a monthly statement, rolling forward as each month passes.

Depending upon your business, collections (business to business) and cash sales (business to consumers) are by far the most difficult items in the forecast and certainly the most critical. You will be more accurate at the beginning of the process than for eight or ten months out. Once you get several months under your belt, you can use these months to project future months with more accuracy. The fact is that this forecast is going to change regularly—depending on sales and general traffic to your store or website. (If you have a retail store, you might want to keep track of the traffic and the number who come in who actually buy; the analytical tools on a website allow you to do the same.)

The other categories on your cash flow forecast are not as critical and, in fact, may not apply at all. Most new businesses do not have rents, interest income, or other sources of revenue besides sales generated by the business.

Your next step is to look at the outflows of cash in your forecast. What you will pay suppliers is tricky and requires some work. You have to make a sales forecast and then project your inventory needs to that forecast. You need to understand your purchasing cycle, how long it takes to produce goods (or services), and what your payment policies are. (Often you can arrange special terms with vendors, once they get to know you and understand your business.)

Wages and overhead both should be fairly predictable. Remember to factor in any new hires you plan to make as well as any increases you may give to employees (or to yourself!). Rent, utilities, and the rest of what fits into the overhead category are known to you. Recurring financial obligations, such as interest and debt repayment, may have some variation but typically are straightforward and known well in advance. (You may decide to pay down more of your loan or line of credit than you have to; but you would do that only if your forecast indicates that you will have the cash flow to do this without hurting the business.)

Long-Term Cash Flow Forecasting

Once again, needs depend on your business, but assuming that it is not a part-time one-person affair run out of the basement, you may need a long-term cash flow forecast. If you plan to grow the business significantly, if your business is capital intensive (manufacturing, production, distribution), or if your business is growing faster than anticipated, you do need a long-term cash flow forecast.

This kind of forecast really belongs in your business plan and is directly related to your strategic planning process. Because neither the business plan nor your strategic planning are static, you will constantly change this long-term cash forecast. You may have reasons to expand faster than originally planned; or the business may not allow you to expand at the rate you first thought. Economic conditions change; key employees may leave; bank financing may be difficult to get—there are a host of conditions that may affect your long-term planning and your cash flow requirements as well.

So how long is long-term planning? Generally it is impossible to plan much beyond three years. Some bankers and investors ask for a five-year plan. You can assemble this if it is required, knowing that year three is probably a guess and years four and five are an absolute mystery. If you need it as a requirement, obviously do it. If not, stick with three years.

Trying to estimate (guess) your cash requirements years ahead is not easy, but your chances of doing a good job are directly tied to a good business plan and an ongoing strategic planning process. They fit hand and glove. Don't be surprised if your business changes over time; you start in one direction but find that the real business is over there—something you did not at first anticipate.

As a rule, plan on reviewing and changing if necessary the long-term cash forecast when you work on your annual budget. Most of the cash you receive will be directly tied to your sales; with experience, you will know what to expect in terms of sales and thus your ongoing cash position. Your operating income tends to be a fixed percentage of sales and is stable over time—unless you have some extraordinary expense that could never be anticipated.

The key to grasping long-term cash needs is to understand as well as possible your liquidity, or net working capital. *Working capital* is the difference between short-term assets (cash, inventory, receivables) and short-term liabilities. In accounting terms, *short-term* means in twelve months or less; either assets can be converted to cash or liabilities have to be paid within that period. For most companies the biggest item in this mystery is accounts receivable; and the most important part about accounts receivable is when you will get paid.

One method to project accounts receivable is the flow-of-funds calculation, which tells you how long it takes, on average, to collect each dollar of receivables. For example, if your collection time normally stands at about 27 days, you simply divide forecasted sales by 365 and then multiply by 27 to obtain projected accounts receivable.

You can apply the same principle to accounts payable and inventories by substituting the cost of goods sold for sales. First, divide cost of goods sold for the most recent year by 365 to obtain an average day's cost of goods sold. Then divide that figure into accounts payable and inventories to arrive at days payable outstanding and days inventory outstanding, respectively. Finally, multiply these figures by the average day's cost of goods sold to make your projections.

Now the other side of the ledger: try to estimate your long-term cash needs, which typically are of two kinds—working capital, and payments for financial obligations. In the first case, you are tracking your decrease in accounts payable and any increases in inventories as well as any increases in accounts receivable. In the latter case, you are anticipating any taxes due, interest payments, debt reduction, and capital improvements (e.g., new equipment, new truck). You know ahead of time what your interest expense is going to be, and you can anticipate any tax payments; decisions about paying down debt or making capital improvements are both up to you. You can spend this money or not, depending on whether you anticipate having the resources to do so. This is why long-term forecasting is so important. Equipment wears out, you can outgrow your space—these are changes in your business you need to plan for.

Billing and Collections

As a small business owner, you need to be concerned about billing and collections. These are the basics for a cash management system, and every entrepreneur must both understand these principles and follow them religiously. The fact of the matter is that billing and collections can be some of the most mundane and uninspiring tasks in your business. Face facts: if an account is in arrears, it is often difficult to make a call to try to get paid. Newly minted entrepreneurs hate to make these calls. It will get easier with time and repetition.

Your bank is happy to sell cash management services, for a fee of course, but there are other ways you can improve the chances of prompt payment. Build an online billing system that allows customers to pay by direct deposit; your bank can set this up for you and add a charge for this service. Naturally, it is essential these days to take all major debit and credit cards as well as PayPal. Even if your office is in your home, you can use handheld devices to read credit cards. If you are still using snail mail, remember that the U.S. Postal Service is under a great deal of financial pressure. How it processes mail now may not be the same in a year or two. Check with the local postmaster on the details of mail processing at your post office, then follow these general tips:

- ▶ Mail invoices according to the dispatch priorities of the post office. To take advantage, process invoices to distant customers first. This speeds delivery of these invoices without delaying the delivery of bills to overnight areas.
- ▶ Coordinate invoice mailing with dispatch times at your post office. If your post office mails at noon, 2 p.m., and 5 p.m., get invoices to third-day areas to your post office by noon to guarantee that they do not wait a day at the post office while it processes local mail.
- ▶ Don't use business reply envelopes for incoming customer payments. The post office tends to accumulate such envelopes, delivering them in bunches. This can add a day or more to your collection period, and you pay the postage.

- Use so-called courtesy reply envelopes for incoming payments. The post office does not mass these envelopes for delivery. Meanwhile, you can speed the delivery of these bills to the appropriate in-house employees by adding bar codes, identification marks, or color coding to the envelopes.
- Direct customer payments to a post office box. This eliminates the extra time required for regular delivery by a mail carrier.
- Consider using a lockbox through your bank. Checks are mailed to the box, your bank processes them right away, and you get a report of who paid so you can bring your bookkeeping up to date.

On the flip side of the coin, slow disbursements while maintaining your credit rating in these ways:

- Use express mail for large, just-in-time payments. This allows your company to retain its funds for as long as possible without paying late fees or missing a trade discount.
- Use your own envelopes when paying bills. In many cases, this tactic causes your check to wander for an extra day through your creditor's collection system.
- Mail payments so that they arrive on Friday. Your company retains credit for the funds in its bank account for the weekend.

One of the biggest problems for small businesses is the quality of their customers. If you extend credit to a client, you had better know something about him. Checking credit of customers is routine in all businesses who allow customers to pay in 30 days (the typical arrangement). Some simple steps:

- ▸ Insist on getting referrals of other businesses that have granted credit to a client.
- ▸ Take the time to make the calls—all of them. You will not know what is going on until you ask.
- ▸ Insist that new customers with limited or poor credit history pay upfront—at least part of the invoice.
- ▸ Ask for a credit card as backup; call the issuing company to make sure that it is good and that the customer is not at her credit limit.
- ▸ Ask for better payment terms than the normal 30 days; some companies pay small invoices in 15 days or less—but you have to ask. This is especially true for larger corporations and if your invoice is relatively small.
- ▸ If your client has a short credit history (or none at all), insist on a personal guarantee from the owners. If the company does not pay, they as individuals must pay.

Making Collection Calls

For new business owners, two of the most difficult tasks are cold calling and making collection calls. Both require that you take direct action in an area you are unfamiliar with; in fact, both activities are one and the same: selling. In the first you are trying to get new business; in the second you are trying to get paid and retain your business.

The normal routine for collections is something like this: Immediately after an account is past due (not next week), send out a statement electronically. This rarely results in payment, but it does serve to remind them that money is due. People tend not to pay on statements, only on invoices. Instead, use the tactic of a simple handwritten note on the original invoice, saying "Past due, please pay." Scan it and send it by e-mail. Ten days later, send a second copy with the same message. When the account gets to be 20 days past due, make a polite phone call. It is absolutely imperative that you keep full and complete records for collections: when past-due notices were sent and to whom. Before you send the notices, you may want to find out who pays the bills. Sending notices to the person who bought your goods or services is not going to help you get paid. The notices should go to accounts payable, preferably with a specific name.

On the first call, remember that your tasks are both to collect the money and to keep the customer. There is absolutely no reason to be hostile, angry, or upset. Nor should you be timid, afraid, or uncertain. Have your facts before you. Make sure that you have dates, invoice numbers, and amounts ready. It is a simple business call: an open invoice is 22 days past due; the amount is $450; two notices were sent; when will the invoice be paid?

Don't let the customer put you off with a vague response; "sometime next week" is not acceptable. Ask for a specific date. Keep records of everything that is said so that, if you have to call again, you can repeat what was agreed to. Ask if the customer needs a copy of the invoice faxed or scanned and sent by e-mail. Ask if there was a problem: perhaps the goods were never delivered, or the service was incomplete, or the billing was not as agreed.

The second collection call is the hardest, because if you did the first one right you got a specific agreement to pay and the customer has not done so. Find out why the payment was not made as agreed. Press for details; you have a right to know. Politely insist that the invoice is past due and you would appreciate payment. Ask if there are cash flow problems. Ask for a partial payment and a schedule for the rest of the invoice to be paid. (You really don't want to do this, but something is better than nothing.) Ask for a credit card number to cover the invoice. If you still are not getting a firm commitment to pay, ask for the owner or senior person in charge. Log names, titles, commitments, dates, comments, and all the details.

Suppose that under a 30-day arrangement an invoice is paid by day 60. Is this a bad account? Probably not. This company is doing exactly what you would do—delaying payment as long as possible. However, if you do business with this customer again—and you should try—emphasize that you must have payment by 30 days. Condition the customer to pay on time when the order is taken: Be polite, businesslike, and firm. If the offer for a credit card does not work, ask if they want to transfer the funds by wire. When you invoice clients, make sure the payment terms are clearly stated and in bold. Post your terms where they can be seen, not at the bottom of the invoice in 6-point type.

You may have to decide whether an open invoice is worth chasing after it is 90 days old. Most banks with whom you have a loan will say that any invoices older than 90 days are not collectible and therefore are no longer security for your loan. (This assumes that the bank has secured your business loan with the company's accounts receivable—and it would be rare that they would not.) Remember, there are industry differences—so don't write it off if it is customary to pay after 60 days or later. On the other hand, don't use up valuable time and effort to collect something that clearly is not going to be paid. Write the invoice off and make sure that you don't do business with that customer again.

Also, you have to decide which late invoices are even worth collection calls. You can easily spend $100 worth of company time, plus phone calls and postage, to collect a $15 invoice. What is the point? If the invoice is small, send a notice or two—and if you are not paid, write it off. It is too small to call and collect.

Extending Credit

The best way to prevent collection problems is to have a credit policy. This may seem odd to many small businesses struggling to find and keep clients. But remember the old saying: a sale is not a sale until the money is in the bank. Trying to establish credit limits and controls is a real balancing act. If you are too loose, you will not get paid. If you are too strict, you lose business. A new company cannot afford to lose business, so you should tend to be more willing to take the risk of higher credit until you learn more about the customer.

Your firm's marketing strategy should have an important influence on credit policy. A volume-based marketing strategy calls for a liberal credit policy. On the other hand, selling big-ticket items to a small customer base requires a restrictive policy. If profit margins on your products or services are normally low, your credit policies are of necessity strict; one customer who does not pay will really hurt your overall performance—especially if it is a large amount. If your unit prices (costs of goods sold) are low, you can often get by with a uniform policy covering all of your customers because the risk in actual dollars is small on any one customer. The exception, of course, is the very large customer, who should be treated differently.

Most new companies do not have a credit department. The best approach is to ask for payment in advance, use credit and debit cards, and just use common sense when dealing with large orders or customers that seem shaky or poorly managed. It is not easy to set policies, but it is even more difficult to collect from a poor (literally) client.

Here are some general rules of thumb about granting credit:

▸ The longer a customer company has been in business, the better chance you have of collecting from it.

▸ It is easy to get financial information on publicly held companies.

▸ Ask for and get credit references.

▸ Ask the owners of a small business to guarantee payment personally.

▸ Make sure the company has a checking account, not just the owner's bank account.

▸ Use a collection agency, but only if matters get really ugly. Remember that these agencies take a good chunk of the amount due, so it does not make sense to use these services for small open invoices.

Hard Times

Very few businesses don't go through hard times; many never survive beyond a difficult period. The causes that threaten most small businesses are usually lack of customers, lack of cash, or both. But there can be other severe problems as well:

illness of the owner/manager
divorce or other family problems
substance abuse by an important team member
overly optimistic expectations
overspending

sloppy bookkeeping and poor records management

financial fraud

failure to get competitive bids on products and services

excessive inventory

insufficient inventory (especially in retail)

loan called by a bank

lack of credit from vendors

loss of initiative and interest on the part of management

This list could go on and on. Although it is not the purpose of the book to address all of these issues, there are some prudent and simple financial safeguards that can be used during a crisis period but actually would form the backbone for a management philosophy that could govern your business activities on a permanent basis.

One of the most basic concepts is to start from the beginning and always have a reserve fund for emergencies or for a time of poor sales. This means that when you start the business, and if you assume you need $150,000 to begin operations, you actually secure $200,000 (or more). Additionally, as your sales and collections build, reserve 5 percent or more on a quarterly basis. Do this by postponing capital improvements, delaying sales or marketing programs, using older computers, not adding staff—whatever it takes.

Employees are the most expensive part of any business. By the time you pay actual wages and factor in the costs of benefits, the downtime from vacation and sick days (these all are quantifiable costs), and government-mandated retirement and disability programs, a $40,000-a-year employee really costs you something in the $60,000–$70,000 range. The alternative is to staff your organization, especially in the early stages, with independent contractors. You may end up paying more per hour, but if you don't need them for a full 40-hour week you don't have to pay them.

Learn to negotiate and negotiate hard. This is true when buying inventory or services, it is true with your banking relationships, and it is certainly true when hiring employees or independent contractors. Get competing bids and look at the differences in price, quality, and fulfillment time. Put these data on a spreadsheet and take the time to quantify each aspect of a bid or quote.

In times of crisis, offer customers discounts on their invoice if they pay sooner than the stated terms; a common strategy is 2 percent off if paid in 10 days. More important, work the accounts receivables hard—making sure that every account is paid as close to on-time as possible.

Talk to your creditors and banker. Don't pretend there is not a problem. Be upfront and discuss what you can and cannot do and what the outlook might be. You may have to decide whether the business is viable or not. It may be time to close your business and take your losses, even file for corporate bankruptcy. If the objective advice is that the business is viable, but you are going through a really slow period, you may have to add more cash to the business or find investors. Remember the rule: bankers will never lend to you in a time of crisis; they will not bear the risk. If you are providing a bridge loan to the company from your personal funds, formalize the loan—putting it in writing and make the transaction transparent. This is just one more reason why it is so important to have your own personal financial house in order before starting a business.

Most owner/entrepreneurs take the hit in hard times: reduced or eliminated salary and benefits. If you have employees (rather an independent contractors), it becomes even more difficult if you have to ask for concessions from them—or even let people go. Be frank with your employees; they know there is a problem, so why not discuss the situation in an unemotional and businesslike way.

Ask for their help and even their advice. Ask them to help you focus on reducing expenses: travel, office supplies, new equipment, furniture, conferences—anything that can be postponed should and must be.

Once you have expenses and receivables under as much control as possible, you must focus your attention on the core business: selling your products and services. You need more customers and you need them quickly. You may be tempted to discount in order to drive more volume, but this usually backfires; when the environment improves, it is impossible to pass on price increases because customers are used to your current pricing model. Look for ways to add value, and work the phones looking for new clients or ways to build the business back up.

Resources

FindLaw

Although FindLaw is a site about finding lawyers, it does offer some good advice and content on cash management for small businesses: http://smallbusiness.findlaw.com/business-operations/accounting/accounting-cash-management.html.

Free Management Library

The Free Management Library is a generally content-rich site, covering not only cash management but a host of management issues for both for-profit and not-for-profit companies. The list of topics is truly impressive: www.managementhelp.org.

Microsoft Business Hub

Many readers will find the tools and resources here useful: http://microsoftbusinesshub.com/. For information relevant to new business start-ups, select "Start Your Business" from the solutions drop-down menu on the navigation bar at the top.

TEN

Marketing and Public Relations Basics

Things to know before starting a business:

- ▶ *Everyone in the organization is a marketer.*
- ▶ *Social networking is the most important trend in marketing.*
- ▶ *Social networking is not the only way to market products and services.*
- ▶ *Pricing is the most important function within marketing.*
- ▶ *Discounting is rarely a good strategy, even in hard times.*
- ▶ *A company name that tells the world what you do is priceless.*

The Basics

One of best known international business groups, the American Marketing Association, describes marketing this way: "Marketing is an organizational function and a set of processes for creating, communicating, and delivering value to customers and for managing customer relationships in ways that benefit the organization and its stakeholders." No doubt your reaction is "That's nice—a good solid academic start to a discussion of marketing." But if you take a moment to take this description apart and put it in language that small-business owners understand, there are some important concepts:

▸ "Marketing is an organizational function" means that everyone in the company is a marketer, not just the people in the marketing or customer service departments. Every time you answer a phone call or e-mail, you market your company.

▸ A "set of processes" means that there is a method to this madness—in fact, a lot of money is spent making it all work.

▸ "Creating, communicating, and delivering value" reflects the need to be constantly at work telling current and future customers why you are better, cheaper, higher tech—whatever your value proposition is.

▸ "Managing customer relationships" is, again, everyone's job. Customer calls, the packaging of your product, the look of the catalog, an effective online presence—everything that customers see, hear, or otherwise perceive is geared to their needs.

▸ The "benefit of the organization" is not just making the boss rich but ensuring that good-quality jobs and creative employment flourish.

▸ And finally, "stakeholders": the owners, of course, are stakeholders; but so are the employees, the lending bank, vendors offering credit, and even the customers who depend on your business to provide high-quality and reliable goods and services.

This, in essence, is what marketing is about, whether you are a huge international conglomerate or a newly formed company struggling to find its market and customer niches. The essentials are the same; the execution can be radically different.

The Four Ps (or Seven)

Every student taking Marketing 101 in college hears the "Four Ps" over and over again: product, price, place, and promotion. A famous marketing professor from Harvard, Jerome McCarthy, coined the name Four Ps and discussed them as the essential "marketing mix." Since that time, with the advent of services as opposed to products, three new Ps have been added to the jargon: people, process, and physical evidence.

At first glance, this may seem rather theoretical and hardly the stuff of entrepreneurship. But don't be fooled. Successful companies have modeled their marketing strategy on these concepts. There is a good deal to be learned and much money to be saved by examining and applying this material. Naturally, the application of the Ps is different depending on whether you are using Twitter

What's in a Name?

Naming a business is never easy, especially if you sell directly to the public. A company name should be clever and memorable, but it must also make sense. A company name often is less important for a business-to-business enterprise; "T&J Enterprises" may make little impact, but once your business clients know what you do they can figure it out. But the same name used for a consumer product business is both boring and poor marketing. What enterprise are you in, one has to ask. "T&J" Pet Supplies is also boring, but it at least tells the consumer what you are offering. A personal favorite is a butcher shop/grocery called Moo and Oink. You remember it easily, get a laugh out of the name—especially when they advertise on television with their silly cow and pig caricatures—and it tells you what business they are in.

Naming is so critical that before you even print a flyer or incorporate a business you need to get the name right. Consider some of these issues:

- Is the name hard to say on the phone? Using the last name of the founder is often done with some peril, unless the name is Smith or Jones.
- Does it make sense? One company sold legal forms and called itself Socrates; what does an ancient philosopher have to do with legal forms?
- If you are a sole proprietor running a mini-business from the back bedroom, don't add "associates" to the name. Everyone knows that it is just you. Call it The Smith Company rather than Smith and Associates.
- Abbreviations can be difficult to understand and to associate with a kind of business; they can also be difficult to say. If Rand Computer Consulting Services becomes RCCS, what does that mean? How do you say it?
- Keep it simple.
- Don't try to use a takeoff of a major company name. McDonall Burger Stand will bring a lawsuit for trade name infringement from one of the biggest companies in the world. Corporations have spent billions over the years building their names and protecting their trademarks. Don't believe for a moment that you are too small to go after.
- Naming your company after a relative or spouse might work—like Wendy's, after the founder's daughter. As a rule, though, don't try this unless you are more specific. Kathy's Kitchen Gadgets gets you in good with Kathy and also tells the world what your business is.

or a physical store to communicate your marketing message. But behind it all are the simple concepts.

Product

What is your product (or service) really all about? Is it a cheaper copy of a best-selling widget? What features and benefits resonate with the buyer? It is important to make this connection. It may be as simple as size, color, added benefits, convenience, or even pricing. It satisfies a real or felt need in the buyer. Add-ons such as warranties, guarantees, and servicing help build customer attachment.

Being objective about your product or service is difficult. You need to ask customers or potential customers, using interviews, surveys, focus groups, comparisons with the competition, your advisors—everything and everyone you can get your hands on to help you be realistic about what you plan to sell and what real benefit it is to your buyers. Car manufacturers literally buy their competitors' products and take them apart piece by piece to study innovation and production changes.

Most new companies cannot afford to hire professionals to conduct extensive research about product quality or service advantages. The same is true for focus groups, the fees for which can run up to tens of thousands of dollars. One possible solution is to conduct your own survey using online software like Survey-Monkey. You can generally join for free, though there is a service fee. SurveyMonkey has numerous templates you can use, or you can customize a questionnaire to customers and qualified leads.

A survey can be sent as an attachment to an e-mail as well as printed for use in your store or when visiting clients. Sites like SurveyMonkey offer help in designing your survey, collecting the responses, and analyzing results. Of particular interest is the need to handle bias; questions can be framed to make sure you don't just elicit the answers you want to hear. You can create dozens of types of questions—numerical rankings, multiple choice, rating scales, drop-down menus, and more. The important caveat is *garbage in, garbage out.*

Once you have specifics for your product or service definition, it is important to keep one or two themes before customers all the time. Repeat and repeat again the benefits—whether technology, price, service, or quality. Stay on message until you can determine that there is a new and better message needed. Watch McDonald's commercials; whether price, value, or a new product—or the reintroduction of a classic—they pound home the same message for a particular campaign. Then they move to the next one and repeat the process all over again in a variety of media.

Price

Setting a price for your product is difficult, especially when you compete with larger, more entrenched firms. Marketers and product managers spend months agonizing over pricing; there are fixed and variable costs to cover, pressure from the salespeople to price as cheaply as possible (easier to sell that way), and what the ever-present competition is doing. Pricing is often related to production; this is *cost-based pricing.* If you manufacture 10,000 items at a time, the savings are not as substantial as if you make 100,000 units, so you can charge less the more you make—unless, of course, you make more than you can sell. In that sad situation, you have too much inventory at too low a price, and the only way to get rid of the inventory is to slash prices further. All of this is some version of cost-based pricing, where your primary consideration is what it costs to produce goods or services and how you price them accordingly.

Some companies use a *premium pricing strategy* whereby you set the price higher than your competition. This pricing strategy can be related to the relative perceived value of a product or service. The higher the price, the higher value is placed on it. In other words, your pricing strategy may have nothing to do with the costs of production as discussed above. High-end consumer goods like those from Coach, Hermés, and Tiffany use this model. Although the goods sold by these companies are clearly superior to those sold by mass-market sellers, their pricing strategy has nothing to do with cost, only with the perceived value of the name. What consumer would not feel that a diamond ring from Tiffany is better than one purchased at Target? Pricing, in this case, comes down to your ability to find a number that consumers are willing to pay that is consistent with their perceived value of the offering.

Another pricing strategy is called *cost plus profit*, which is similar to the cost-based pricing just discussed. In this case, however, you have a predetermined profit number—a percentage that is typical in your industry. You gather all of the costs—fixed and variable—and then determine what you need or want as a profit margin, which you add to the back end of the price to ensure profitability. This approach sounds good in theory but may be difficult to implement.

Market-based pricing is determined by studying all of your competitors' pricing strategies and how customers decide what and when to buy in order to fix the price of your offering. You need to gather as much data as possible, both internally and externally, to make pricing decisions. You need real, hard data on the cost of goods sold—not just estimates. Further, remember that shipping, some fixed overhead, and other variables might be included in the real cost of goods sold. Your markup has to be high enough to cover costs and low enough to compete, based on the features and benefits you offer.

Some companies choose a *market penetration* pricing strategy; this approach is most commonly used to introduce a new product or product line. The intent is to grab market share quickly. This kind of pricing involves lowering your price to a level below your competition's to gain immediate name recognition and to attract your competitor's buyers. Once buyers have been acquired and become comfortable or attached to the new product or service, a company may gradually increase the price to equal that of the competition.

Whatever your theoretical approach to pricing, the simple fact is that many new companies are forced to accept dismal markups because they are not large enough and do not have economies of scale in their favor. If you sell 100 hours of service at $500 per hour (total revenue of $50,000) and you have four employees, the productivity per worker can be measured in dollars: $12,500 per person. If, on the other hand, lowering your pricing to $350 per hour results in 225 billed hours, the gross profit is $78,750, with your productivity per person increasing substantially to $19,687 per person. Plus you now have nearly $30,000 more to cover fixed costs such as rent and utilities. Test and test again to find the right price, and don't be afraid to change prices—including increasing them. In some industries, marketers actually increase prices for older salable inventory; the rationale is that they are going to sell the same amount of old stuff whether it costs 10 percent more or not; there is no price sensitivity. So why not improve margins.

When, not if, economic times turn hard, a knee-jerk reaction is to start discounting in order to keep customers or increase market share. *Discounting* for this discussion means across-the-board financial incentives to buy goods or services—not a one-time sale to reduce obsolete inventory but a strategic move in response to the perceived inability or unwillingness of customers to buy at your current pricing structure. It may seem a good idea at the time, but when you discount you start down a slippery slope. The airline industry in the late 1990s is one of the finest examples of discounting, offering reduced fares and incentives to fill planes; the problem is that the margins were reduced so badly that most of the major carriers ended up in bankruptcy—and that was before the prices of crude oil and refined diesel fuel went sky high.

What are some of the results of discounting?

> ▶ It reduces gross margins and profitability, thus limiting cash flow.
> ▶ Poor cash flow means that a company is dependent on new lines of credit or other cash infusions until the market improves.
> ▶ It may be impossible to return to former prices. Customers get used to the discounted prices and refuse to buy when you go back to the old pricing.
> ▶ Discounting may cheapen the brand, causing customers to think of your services or goods as having lesser quality.

The alternative to discounting is adding value to the customer's purchases: extended warranties, more and better service, free delivery, or a discount on the next purchase. Further, marketing has to stress the value proposition: why the customer needs your products and services.

Promotion

For most nonmarketers, promotion seems to be the primary function of the marketing manager. Promotion is all about publicity, sales promotion, the website, Facebook presence, advertising, catalogs, brochures, personal selling, and branding. Remember, branding is a means of promoting not only a product or service but your company as well. Think of how much money is spent in a year by major consumer companies just to keep their name (brand) before the public.

For small companies, promotion costs a lot in proportion to revenue. Although the costs of designing and hosting a website have come down dramatically, they are still an expensive (time and money) proposition. If there is any activity that must be done correctly, it is making use of a website. It is beyond the scope of this book to detail the specifics of good promotion through a website, but a few obvious major issues can be mentioned:

- ▶ The website must be designed for clear objectives. Is it for information (promotion), or for e-commerce (selling), or both?
- ▶ The site should be appropriate to the product or service; if you are a financial consulting business, your site ought to have a rich, businesslike look to it. Bunnies, flowers, and cute typefaces would be inappropriate.
- ▶ It must be easy to navigate; three clicks should get you to the cart.
- ▶ It must be clear: what are you selling, and for what price?
- ▶ An enriched site does better; offer free content, checklists, articles, or other advice that will keep customers on your site. The longer they are there, the better chance you have of getting business.
- ▶ The more textual content you have, the better chance you have of catching customers through keyword searches.

▸ Use simple, clean graphics and images. Don't flash in the customer's face.

▸ Any partners or other sites you link to must share your values; if they are perceived as inappropriate or amateurish, you will be too.

▸ Spelling, grammar, and syntax need to be perfect.

▸ Make the site simple but easy to navigate.

▸ When in doubt, see what the real pros do—like Amazon.com.

▸ Ask customers for feedback and, before you go live, get as many people as you can to test your site and offer reactions.

Although a website is essential, and seemingly the most important part of promotion, some of the old standards are equally fundamental. Publicity is a crucial part of promotion: it is both very effective and relatively inexpensive. Read the business and professional publications religiously and profile how people manage to get their name, company, and brand in articles, interviews, on television and radio, and in blogs. The key to success for a small business is selfless promotion through publicity.

Write an electronic newsletter, offer tips of the day or week, or send an e-mail blast once every few weeks. Just don't punish your customers with too much in their in-boxes; be judicious in the use of these kinds of electronic messages. Limit the size of the newsletter to a screen or two. You can always add hot links to a longer message or article for readers who may want more information. Tweet with important new information or benefits to your customers. Start a blog instead of the newsletter, but know that blogging takes a lot of time and there are hundreds of thousands of blogs out there. It is difficult to get a following unless you have something terribly insightful (or controversial) to say. Remember, of course, that you want to make a clear relationship between the message sent and what you do. Display your tag line, company name, phone, fax, and e-mail address clearly. This kind of publicity, whether printed or electronic, can be used for almost any kind of small business—from retail to consulting.

The physical business is, in itself, your biggest advertisement and promotion—thus location is so terribly important. If you cannot be seen or your location is obscure, with little or no foot or automobile traffic, you lose your best promotion. This is why signage, both inside and outside the store, is crucial. You need to communicate a clear, consistent message—not only who you are but also what you do and when you are open. Use lettering that is clever but readable. It is amazing the number of retail signs that are difficult to read (and thus ineffective), with style overriding function.

Many small businesses, often neighborhood restaurants, rely on the old standby: flyers. They are passed out, mailed to houses, included with purchases, stuffed in mailboxes, placed on public bulletin boards—even annoyingly placed on windshields of parked cars. Flyers are cheap, and when used with a promotional special—discount or two-for-one offer—they can drive traffic to your business. They can be used as inserts with local magazines or newspapers. You can also buy into local marketing promotions that send poly-bag promotions from various companies to consumer's homes.

No correspondence, invoice, or shipment should leave your business without your latest catalog or flyer; make every effort to get the current customer to buy again with a special offer, free shipping, discount, or two-for-one sale. This effort can be particularly important if you are introducing new products or services. Tweet and blog the same offers to reinforce the message. Use the open white space on an invoice or packing slip to print out your message.

No opportunity should be wasted to get some message to the customer—either about products or about your company generally.

Some companies, especially if their market is very local—say within five miles of their business—find ads in church or social organization bulletins to be effective. You might sign a contract for six months to a year, and the same advertisement appears every week. This approach can be effective because people like to buy locally and see the value of helping a local church member; it is a very personal way to market. Additionally, the church or organization benefits from earning income for its house bulletin.

The next step, of course, is sponsorships. Place an ad in the program for a street fair or play; buy a booth, even if you are not selling anything. Pay for the uniforms for the local sports team—and get your company name on them and signs at the ballpark or gym. The goodwill you earn is tremendous. But make it clear to everyone that you are not just being charitable; you are expecting to increase your business and gain customers. Ask parents (and the kids) to tell everyone who you are and that you have sponsored them. Don't be shy about this.

There is a huge and growing business of selling promotional items to stores, restaurants, service businesses, and small companies in general. These firms sell everything from motivational signs to flags, banners, key chains, cups, coasters, golf balls, bookmarks, pens, magnets, shopping bags, and a thousand and one other items with your logo, company name, URL, address, and phone number. These companies are very successful for a reason: These promotional giveaways seem to work. They are semipermanent reminders that you are in business and where the customer can find you.

This short primer on marketing would not be complete without a discussion about referrals and the vital importance this task holds in your business life. A referral is nothing more than an introduction or recommendation. It can be very casual and low key. In some professions, say medicine, physicians traditionally have not advertised—although this is changing. A referral was the way a doctor recommended a colleague or a patient recommended a doctor. Of course, this is what Facebook and LinkedIn are all about: making viral connections, talking about products and services, introducing your business to your "associates," and getting the name out generally.

It is not uncommon in professional circles that one of the first points of discussion is "How did you hear about us?" Everyone who is thoughtful about building a business, no matter what kind, is conscious of where they get new clients. The cheapest way to get a customer is through a referral—from a friend, relative, business association, current or former client, vendor, banker, even competing businesses.

There is both an art and a science to getting (and giving) referrals. You can make an informal bargain with a complementary business—you own a pet shop, and someone else has a grooming and walking service. You refer and advertise for the other business, and that company passes out your catalogs, coupons, and flyers to its clients. Simple, but very effective. As you close a sale, mention that if you ever need a groomer for the dog or someone to walk an animal, you know the best person.

Some referrals are spontaneous; you and a friend try a new restaurant, and you tell ten people how much you enjoyed the experience. Three of the ten try it, and they each recommend to five to ten people. And on and on the process goes.

On the other hand, the art and science of getting referrals is often a deliberate process that must be ingrained in your marketing strategy and used and practiced by all of your employees and associates. Spontaneous referrals are wonderful, the icing on the cake, but you cannot depend on them or even expect them unless your customer service is exceptional. Most customer experiences are neither so positive nor so negative as to generate this type of spontaneity. Rather, people have to be prompted, and constantly, to tell others about your products or services. In the financial services business, selling life insurance and mutual funds, lead generation is so critical that agents actually ask clients to write down names of friends, relatives, and colleagues whom the client thinks might be able to use the agent's services. This is a bold, frontal approach to the process of referrals—no subtlety at all; the agent makes it perfectly clear that he cannot do his job without these qualified leads.

Asking for referrals, no matter how it is done, is not easy for most people. You need to be direct and specific; this also assumes that you have offered a good product or service.

TIPS ON ASKING FOR REFERRALS

▸ Always carry business cards (or even a small brochure).

▸ Make sure that your e-mail address and website address are prominent wherever the company name appears.

▸ Even in social situations, people ask what your business does; if you don't belabor it and make them feel uncomfortable, you can tell about your business in a few words (prepare an elevator speech) and pass on a business card.

▸ Assume nothing; ask your banker, accountant, lawyer, and vendors to make referrals, and tell them you will do the same for them.

▸ Ask your existing contacts, leads, customers, and business associates to send referrals your way.

▸ Don't be shy or embarrassed; once you ask a few times, you will get over any hesitation.

- After you complete a transaction, ask the client who else might benefit from your services. Get name and phone number.
- You have to *use* referrals that are given to you; putting them in the drawer won't bring more business. This means cold calls—and the dreaded fear of rejection.
- Referrals have a shelf life longer than most people assume. If you make contact and get no response, follow up with a phone call.
- Even if you were turned down, call or e-mail again in two months.
- Space your direct contacts; you don't want to be a pest. But you can still send a brochure or your e-newsletter between calls.
- If you are not good at cold calling, bring in someone who is.
- Whenever you get positive feedback, ask the customer for permission to quote him in your catalogs and literature or on your website. But don't make up customer names and quotations. They can be spotted easily for what they are—phonies.

One effective method of ensuring referrals is to reward those who sent customers to you. It may be nothing more than a short thank-you note, a discount coupon for their next purchase, or an item of some value—depending on the potential sale that may result from the referral. Be careful about gifts given to corporate employees. Many firms have strict codes of behavior about what their employees can and cannot accept. An inexpensive lunch? No problem. An expensive personal gift or bottle of wine? Maybe not. The point is to reinforce behavior that is beneficial to your company.

Marketing gets the word out about your company, generating leads, qualifying those leads, convincing them that your products and services are superior (or better priced), convincing them to buy, and getting them to come back again—and telling friends and associates about your business. Marketing is also constant and a good deal of work.

Place

The final traditional P usually refers to how the product or service gets to the customer. The simplest example is retail versus online. Obviously, many service business have neither of these options, so place (placement) may refer to your home region or a particular region where you will offer your products and services.

Place also raises the question of whether you need or can get distribution through other, larger channels than your own store or website. Can you work out an arrangement to be sold (represented, or rep'd) by a large wholesaler, or can you sell directly to a big-box store—or even a regional chain? Can you set up a store within a store? Many specialty rug counters in large department stores are actually independent businesses that pay a fee or commission for space and services within the store. For all practical appearances, the rug department is part of the store. In fact, it is not.

Distribution of a new consumer product often starts slowly and very locally. Your formulation for a new body lotion is an innovative product, but you need to get the local shops and boutiques to carry the line. Even the smallest stores will not carry a single product. They want a larger line; it is simply too inefficient and costly to do the paperwork, track sales, and reorder. You can extend a product line by having different sizes and different price points; different flavors, colors, or fragrances; or a second or third product related to the first—maybe hand and foot lotion in addition to your main product.

There are plenty of great success stories of entrepreneurs getting their wares in one or two local shops and working diligently to fill the distribution pipeline with personal visits, phone calls, and mailings. It takes a lot of hard work. Owners are usually the buyers in small shops; even in stores with buyers, getting their attention can be demanding. There is no incentive for a buyer to even look at a new line without significant sales history. And that, of course, is the problem. The distribution has to build, and you cannot use the smallest accounts to convince the larger accounts, because the numbers won't impress them. Ten units a month at the local boutique might seem like a good start to you, but it is peanuts to the buyer for a fifty-store chain.

Expect to lose money and a lot of it while you set up distribution. Accounts will want huge discounts to try the line; they may ask for the right to return the products if they don't sell; they may insist that they pay only when inventory is sold (consignment). And expect that they will pay very slowly—60 to 90 days or more would not be uncommon. You or your assistant, if you are lucky to have one, will have to be cook and bottle washer—managing the sales calls and the accounts, checking on inventory, arranging payment without losing the account, and more. Early distribution tends to be fragile. One miss, poor sales, back-ordered inventory, or billing mistakes, and it will be hard to retain the account. On the other hand, if you sell through at one major account, you have a referral as well a business success story.

Place also suggests something about market segmentation—meaning the primary audience for your products. You may choose to segment young families, older consumers, small businesses—all of which form the place of your marketing strategy. You can roll this all into one ball by deciding that you are going to start a business that is Internet-based only, offering computer services to older adults in your local community. Your plan may be to never go beyond 50 miles of your home base—to limit costs and to concentrate on the most immediately available customers.

Several times in this book the advantages and disadvantages of retailing come up. Please remember that opening a retail store has so many difficulties and costs associated with it that you are forced to do much more planning, analysis, and market research than, say, if you open an online store. This is not to suggest that one is better than the other; much depends on background, whether this is a full-time or part-time business, your financial structure, and your experience in retailing. As you have begun to see, many online businesses expand to retail distribution.

There Is More to the Story Than the Four Ps

Indeed there is. In fact, the basic model just presented is only part of the story, according to some experts. This marketing model was created primarily for consumer product marketing and thus is not particularly useful to industrial (or business-to-business) selling or for marketing services. There is more to the story, and recent marketing experts have added to the list.

The people component is huge in contemporary marketing—not only the initial sales effort but the entire selling, marketing, and servicing process. In fact, any individual—by e-mail, on the phone, in a letter, or in direct contact—is part of the fifth P, people. All major organizations, regardless of size, attempt to control this process to the best of their ability. Employees are continually trained and coached to handle customer relations with kid gloves.

Assuming that the customer relationship is productive (meaning profitable or potentially profitable and not adverse in any major way), retaining current customers must take priority over all other business strategies and patterns. The cost of replacing an existing customer is enormous, and many small firms are dependent on a few customers who make up a large portion of their business. The best advice is to handle them with care. You need and want them for your current business, for future increases in businesses, and as referrals when landing new customers.

An additional component of the marketing matrix that often is not included is another P: process. Essentially process is any standardized behavior or system used to deliver goods and services to clients. Small businesses tend to have fewer established processes; huge corporations have entire libraries of standard operating procedures designed to introduce standardization and uniformity. One of the traditional advantages of small and emerging companies is the ability to adjust midstream in terms of customer relations, delivery of services, or any other defined process. You as an entrepreneur are far more able to adjust to a change of business climate or customer needs. As companies mature, it almost seems as though process becomes more important than actual customer satisfaction.

Create processes only when you need them. Outline for yourself and for your employees the basics, then train them around these basics. Adding layers of process, forms, checklists, or other functions does not make money. Selling and delivering satisfaction to the customer does make money.

If your company consults on human resource issues, it is almost impossible to demonstrate your skills and expertise without actually doing the work for the client. But on your website and in your brochures you can list former satisfied clients, diagram and describe your consulting style (visually rather than verbally), list specific improvements or cost savings from your work (without identifying clients), and post quotes as testimonials to your effectiveness.

Branding

One of the strongest trends in marketing is the emphasis on branding. Branding is nothing more than the collective images, impressions, and symbols of your company and your products or services. Your brand may include a logo, trademarks, the company name, or the typeface and colors used on products, promotional materials, packaging, and advertising. Branding includes any saying, slogans, songs, or caricatures (the Pillsbury Doughboy) that are used to convey a message to the audience.

Branding is used effectively by large corporations, some of which spend literally billions each year not only promoting their brands but protecting them. Smaller businesses want to spend their marketing dollars to make customers aware of their products and their companies, thus creating a brand identity: "Oh, you are that cute little company that sells . . . "

Branding begins with a company name, a slogan, product design, and packaging and should be carried out with every attempt to use media and create an impression. Standardize everything to match, even your business cards. If you used green and pink in your logo, the color combo is part of your identity. Even the sign in front of the store and the walls within need to be the same green and pink.

Branding ultimately is a signal to consumers that they can have confidence in a product or service because they have used it before with satisfaction or others have used it. Branding connotes value, comfort; a brand also takes a long time to gain acceptance. But start from the beginning to brand both your company and your products.

Finally, if you are not already, go green. It is all the rage, and it is a trend that is not going to go away. But promote your green business only if you really are ecology-conscious. Consumers are used to businesses that shout green but don't act it. But give your customers choices. Don't insist that they bring their own bags into the store to take goods home. Buy equipment, inventory, supplies, and other business necessities that are earth-friendly and let your customers know about it. Be aware, though, that if you go green, you may find that costs go up, and you may have to pass those costs on to your customers.

Getting Noticed

The whole point of marketing and public relations is to get noticed; customers cannot buy from you if they don't know you exist. Fortunately, there are many inexpensive ways to increase awareness. The new art form of blogging is one of them. Some people are absolutely addicted to blogging, so be aware that if you get a successful blog going, it may take a good deal of time and attention.

Small companies can set up free accounts on WordPress.com or Blogger.com. To attract an audience, your blog has to be more than just an advertisement of your company or services. You need interesting, sometimes provocative, content; in this wider context, you can weave in information about your company and products. Be active in other blogs and provide links to your blog. The more links, the better chance of getting attention. But do remember the caution that blogging can become addictive: you do not make money per se from blogging; rather, it is a means to an end.

Another inexpensive and effective promotional strategy is presentation, whether speaking, teaching, or writing. There is no better and quicker way to get a name for yourself and your business than by being present to your client base. Many small-business owners find that giving free seminars or participating in continuing education or being active in a professional society builds their reputation as experts in the field and the people to be hired or contracted to assist with a project or a problem.

Writing in trade journals, industry publications, or even the local newspaper can give you tremendous exposure. Better yet, write a book. You instantly become the expert in the field. When meeting prospective clients for the first time, include your articles or a copy of the book in your portfolio of marketing and presentation materials. It follows quite naturally that writing leads to interviews on radio, television, or online media. This kind of exposure is invaluable.

Consider putting in place loyalty programs that reward and encourage your current customers to come back more often. Offer a frequent-buyers club, with specials, discounts, extra service, and free products or samples. Your goal is to create a kind of emotional attachment between your products and services and your company.

Blogging and e-mails, surveys, and web blasts can all be effective marketing campaigns, but you may not be exploiting the Internet for its full potential by just using these strategies. Put together a useful but entertaining video about your company and post it to YouTube or similar sites. If the video has any punch at all, people will pick up on it and send it to friends, who send it to more friends. This is an effective way to get your name out there.

You can get your company listed on free websites such as Del.icio.us (www.delicious.com), Digg.com, Squidoo (www.squidoo.com), and Yelp.com; the trick is to get family, friends, loyal customers, employees—even vendors—to tout your name and the quality of your services. Don't forget places like Craigslist (www.craigslist.com) and Metromix (www.metromix.com), which often offer free online calendars and list upcoming events. The number of people who regularly use Craigslist is astounding. A little information spread on this site can go a long way to get you noticed.

Resources

SurveyMonkey

For more information, visit www.surveymonkey.com. The site is rich with information for beginners. You can take a complete tour, create surveys, collect data, and analyze it, all without buying the program until you are ready. Further, you have the option to get the basic package for free.

Constant Contact

A site heavily promoted is Constant Contact. According to the website, the company helps small businesses, associations, and not-for-profit companies connect with their customers, clients, and members. Constant Contact offers e-mail marketing and online survey tools to help businesses build professional-looking e-newsletters and conduct surveys. Visit www.constantcontact.com for more information.

ELEVEN

Inventory Basics

Things to know before starting a business:
- ▶ *You can always buy or make more.*
- ▶ *Excess inventory kills cash flow.*
- ▶ *Your online store or cash register can help you manage inventory.*

The Challenges of Managing Inventory

As we often note in this book, it is especially challenging to start or buy and run a business that requires either manufacturing or inventory. If your business model requires inventory—as a retail store, distributor, or Internet seller of products—inventory management is tricky, and mistakes can be costly. Trying to figure out which products to make and in what quantity is maddening. Too little inventory, and you risk losing sales because customers cannot find popular items in your place of business. Too much inventory, or the wrong inventory, is a slippery slope to insolvency.

Here's one basic type of inventory problem. Typically, a business has too much—especially in the start-up phase. Management is optimistic and quickly learns that if you buy in larger quantities the cost of goods per unit (price paid to your supplier) goes down. A simple example will do. Assume your business is reselling high-end picture frames on the Internet; your plan is to have as many as two hundred items in your store. The supplier has minimum order quantities of three of each frame style; any order of five units or more guarantees a substantial reduction in costs—including the advantage of saving shipping and handling from the supplier. The all-glass contemporary frame has a suggested retail price of $55.00; its costs are as follows:

3 units	$29.75 each	Shipping: $11.00
4–10 units	$22.45 each	Shipping: $13.00–$15.00
11–20 units	$19.00 each	Shipping: $15.25–$17.50

If the owner buys at the second pricing level, four to ten units, the savings in cost of goods alone is $7.30 per unit; the gross margin, assuming all units are sold, is $32.55 (55.00 − 22.45) versus a gross margin of $25.25 for each unit if he purchases less than four units. The temptation is to buy in higher volume so as to increase gross margin. The problem is that unsold goods or goods that are eventually discounted in order to get rid of them erode the total gross margin of the entire retail operation terribly. This simple illustration makes the point that purchasing inventory solely on the basis of discounts for quantity or in an attempt to increase gross margins is fraught with peril.

You Can Always Buy or Make More ··

No matter how hard you try, you will never get your inventory purchases in line with customer expectations. It is virtually impossible. As a general rule in starting out, buy smaller quantities of inventory until you test the market and begin to know what customers will and will not buy. You can always buy more. Remember too that your pricing decisions may have a strong impact on sales volume and thus inventory turnover. Your goal is to have the highest amount of turns per month, quarter, or year that you can. A *turn* is an item that is sold and replaced with new inventory. But turns can be deceptive. A car dealership has very different expectations of how much inventory it can turn than an online T-shirt seller.

There are many reasons to have conservative inventory, especially when cash flow is small. The obvious one is that you have a great deal of cash sitting in inventory, and it can be costly to finance. Your vendors do not care if sales are slow; they still expect to be paid in 30 or 40 days. You still have to pay the bank loan, which is loaded with interest and fees. If your cash is tied up with too much inventory, you have less dollars to use on marketing and direct sales. If your inventory is weighted to slow-selling product, you do not have the cash to buy the goods that are selling. It becomes a vicious circle.

It is generally best to think of holding costs in terms of their annual costs. To do this, you need accurate representations of your annual inventory levels. Track inventory month by month and use these values to find the average holding cost, as opposed to averaging the year's beginning and year's end. Do this for finished goods, work in progress, and raw materials.

Figure out what percentage of the total value of the good is being incurred as a holding cost. Cost of capital and opportunity costs should be the first things you think of. If you are financing the goods with a 10 percent loan, then the holding costs are at least 10 percent annually. When you are evaluating the total value, include the value of any labor that has been added to the goods.

Next consider the cost of storage. Based on the inventory you need to carry, how much space do you need, and how much does that space cost per unit as a percentage of each good? Again, determine the insurance cost that should be allocated to each good as a percentage of that good.

Evaluate the probability that goods will deteriorate or otherwise become obsolete, assess the average rate at which this occurs, and use this to quantify the average holding cost per good as a percentage of that good on an annual basis. Are there any other costs incurred simply by being in possession of a good? If you can think of any, treat them as holding costs. Add up all of these percentages, and together they make your holding costs. For example, assume you rent storage space for $5,000, pay insurance to protect your inventory for $150 per year, and pay a part-time employee $10,000 per year to manage this space. Further assume that the goods cost $100,000 and that there is shrinkage (damage, goods stolen) of 5 percent a year. Your total holding costs would be $20,150, or 20 percent ($10,150/$100,000).

Of course, there is the other side of the coin. Have you ever gone into a retail store and found shelves looking bare, with only one or two of each item? Without enough inventory, you can't generate the cash you need to operate a business. Furthermore, a lack of inventory frustrates customers, causing them to cancel online orders or shop elsewhere. Most consumers hate back orders; they do not want to wait a week or two for their goods.

Look at Large Retail Operations for Some Answers

Even the biggest operations have inventory problems, but they also have the tools to ensure that they do not overstock or understock their stores. For one thing, they have inventory-control software to guide their decisions. This kind of software is available for smaller operations, and some applications can be linked to standard accounting packages such as QuickBooks.

The most valuable tool large operations have is the cash register with the capacity to scan a bar code to report what is selling and at what rates. If you set up an Internet store, you can use Google Analytics and other inexpensive tools to analyze your sales and thus make better, prudent inventory decisions. If you have a retail operation, you absolutely want to be able to use the bar coding on the packaging to track sales. This is a costly and time-consuming process to set up, but there are software tools available to help you manage this function. This investment in time and systems will help you understand what is selling and what is not, further helping you control your inventory. (If worst comes to worst, you can always set up a manual system to track what goes out. A crude system is better than guessing.)

If you are planning to buy a franchise, make sure that the franchisor offers this kind of management software. Most do, for they are just as interested in tracking sales and inventory as you are.

Another reason to look at the big-box companies is to see what they do when they have obsolete inventory or too much of a seasonal item, for example. These operations respond immediately and begin discounting merchandise in anticipation of either new models or overstock. Do the same. The opportunity cost of holding too much inventory is too high. If your markups on goods are at least 100 percent (twice the cost you paid), you have substantial room to discount and still have a positive gross profit. As radical as it sounds, it is better to get something for this inventory than nothing at all—which means that even if you take a small loss it is worth moving excess inventory.

Inventory that cannot be sold must be given away or destroyed. At some point, your accountant will inform you that you cannot keep inventory on the books as an asset that is not salable. In most cases, it is best to write off or write down the value of inventory when you are profitable—it reduces any potential tax liability. Don't be timid, as hard as it is to seemingly be throwing away money in the form of inventory. Clean house and learn the lessons of overstocking and poor inventory management.

Just in Time

One of the best management concepts of the past few decades is just-in-time inventory (JIT). Students of business associate this concept with Japanese car manufacturers, which, because they had limited physical space, could not house or store parts and finished cars. Ironically, the concept was first developed by Henry Ford, who asked himself why he should buy or store something until he actually needed it. In this management model, inventory is actually considered a waste, not an asset: money, time, and process are wasted by holding excessive inventory or parts.

JIT inventory management systems are most common in complex manufacturing and warehousing industries, but even small businesses can modify the basic concepts to keep stock low and manageable. The message for small-business owners is to focus on how to have less inventory but have it readily available (just in time) if customers' demand increases.

One of the major principles of JIT is employee empowerment. Essentially, staff members or salespeople on the floor are not just clerks or customer order processors; they are actively involved in what is selling and why. They may be allowed to make purchasing decisions, but at the very least they serve as another set of eyes as to what is going on with your business.

JIT is closely related to vendor relationships. In some large retail operations, the vendors actually manage the inventory of bulk or frequently sold items. Why would a large retailer want to store and manage thousands of pallets of paper towels, for example, when the manufacturer can do it for them? The supplier can "see" into the sales patterns at the stores and has the authority to direct inventory to the appropriate warehouse or directly to the store. The point is that the reseller and the vendor have formed a partnership to manage inventory. Your vendor relationships may not be that sophisticated, but you can work with suppliers to model inventory needs and work out creative arrangements that could include holding inventory until you need it and managing cash flow as well.

If you have a warehouse or even a stockroom in the back of the store, sensible organization of that space is critical to managing inventory. Employees need to be able to find inventory; simple matters such as good signage and a simple spreadsheet (stock locater database) to tell everyone where inventory is stored save time and money. If you are large enough, you may even want to consider outsourcing your warehouse operations; you don't have to staff it, and you don't have to manage the process. Let someone who is an expert in warehousing and fulfillment do this work for you.

Simple Methods of Inventory Control ···················

There are strong advantages to having inventory control systems that monitor movements by recording them at the cash register through scanning and bar codes, but many businesses simply cannot manage such a process or afford to implement this kind of system. There are alternatives for the budding entrepreneur.

Visual control: take a moment each day and physically walk the store or storeroom to see what is selling and make note of what has to be ordered. This system has been used for decades by small stores and shops, and there is no reason it cannot work for you. In some cases, you can physically count your inventory daily or weekly and make buying decisions based on that. Some businesses still use a click control system: as an item is sold, it is recorded manually on a spreadsheet. Finally, many retailers still rely on stub control: a portion of the price tag is removed when an item is sold, telling the owner what needs to be reordered. Manufacturer's reps or salespeople can often be valuable, visiting your location on a regular basis to rotate stock and work with you on your reorder points.

Inventory control can become greatly complicated when you order from more than one supplier—which you will likely have to do. No retail or online store has just one supplier; that would mean that your offerings are limited to what one company produces and at price points that may or may not match your customer profile. If you are buying similar or like goods from two different suppliers, you have the advantage of pitting one against another for your business. Having more than one supplier also ensures that you do not run out of stock at a critical time. But it also means that you have to track current inventory from each and any inventory in transit (or about to be shipped).

Good inventory management also means that you have a clear understanding of how your suppliers work and what lead times (manufacturing, picking, packing, and shipping) are required. In most business environments, inventory needs are uneven—at certain times of the year you need particular goods in larger quantities, and perhaps quicker, in order to anticipate demand. Is it better to have too little inventory than too much? As a start-up, yes, too little is better; you can always back-order or give customers some kind of incentive to take the goods later than they might have wanted.

Some businesses are extremely seasonal: most of their revenue comes in a few months of the year—summer or around the end-of-year holidays. In these cases, inventory management is both critical and difficult. If you run a garden center, how many flats of annuals do you order, and when do you stop ordering because demand slacks off in July? What items do you use to replace the seasonal ones in order to keep some cash flow going through the rest of the year? This is both an inventory issue and a strategic one. A classic example is lawn mower manufacturers. These companies went into the snowblower business to keep their plants running year-round and to balance the seasonality of their product line. What is your version of the snowblower?

If you cannot make these tactics work, another kind of solution to inventory problems is to work with your wholesaler or jobber. If you own an Internet business, you can arrange to have the order filled directly by the manufacturer or wholesaler. It may cost you more, meaning that your gross margin goes down (and probably substantially), but it may be more efficient financially because you stock less inventory. This model works particularly well with high-priced goods or ones that sell slowly but you feel you need to offer.

Resources

QuickBooks

If you use QuickBooks as your accounting solution but need better inventory control, Fishbowl Inventory is a fully integrated inventory system used with QuickBooks. Fishbowl Inventory was one of the first programs to integrate with QuickBooks and currently holds Gold Developer Status, Intuit's highest award for third-party integrators. Unlike most software packages, when you purchase Fishbowl Inventory you get the entire feature set—not just a set of modules. See www.fishbowlinventory.com.

Essentials of Inventory Management and *Inventory Best Practices*

Two books worth reviewing are *Essentials of Inventory Management* (AMACOM, 2011), by Max Muller, and *Inventory Best Practices* (Wiley, 2011), by Steven Bragg. Both serve as good desk references for small-business owners.

TWELVE

Getting Out, Closing Down, Bankruptcy

Things to know before starting a business:

▶ *An exit strategy should be part of your business plan.*
▶ *Even if you fail, you will learn a great deal for your next venture.*

It Happens

The very title of this chapter is a bummer. This is a book about being an entrepreneur, a successful small-business owner. But sadly, as this book began, so shall it end—with the simple reality that not every brilliant idea works out; events, personal and financial, mitigate the enthusiasm and the reality of running a business. This is emotionally draining; you worked so hard to plan and start a business, and you find that it is not growing as you hoped (or need it to do).

If you are paying attention to your business as you should be, testing different concepts, starting it part-time so as not to lose the income and benefits of a present job, the real tragedy is on a psychological level. It can be devastating to see plans, money, and hard work evaporate.

But there is an important caveat to this discussion. Not all businesses close because they fail. A business owner may decide that she is not interested in the entrepreneurial lifestyle. Or, perhaps, the business was started as a stopgap until new or better employment could be found. The plan all along may have been to work for just a few years after retirement, not indefinitely.

Orderly Closing

It would be nice to assume that closing a business is by choice rather than by economic fiat. It would also be nice to simply close the door one day and be finished with it. Unfortunately, it is not so clear-cut. If you choose to close (or sell) the business, you have time to manage the process and recover as much cash as possible through a voluntary liquidation of assets and goodwill.

What follows are the basics, whether the closing is voluntary or involuntary:

1. Vote to dissolve. The owners (or a majority of them, if your rules so allow) of the business entity must all agree to dissolve the company. Your articles of incorporation, partnership agreement, or articles of organization should contain provisions that set the rules for such

a vote. If not, state or local statutes that govern your form of business act as fallback provisions by prescribing how a vote to dissolve must be conducted.

2. Put a dissolution team together. This team should include your attorney, accountant, and a business valuation expert if you plan to sell the business. If the company is larger, include the chief financial officer and any key operating managers. This, of course, can get tricky, for they will need to find other employment. They also may be candidates to buy the business—either outright or through a leveraged buyout (using the company's assets and future cash flow to pay you for the business).

3. List assets and take inventory. This is essential for the business valuation and is necessary in order to file your business's final tax returns. For many businesses, this is a simple task; for others, this process could take months.

4. Get a business valuation. A valuation, though costly, may prevent future disputes from arising among the business's owners and provide evidence to justify the figures you use on your final tax return. This valuation also could be the starting point in selling your business; naturally, potential buyers will get their own valuations (always less than yours) as part of their negotiation strategy.

5. Set a timetable. Be realistic. Closing a business takes time. Developing reasonable time frames for each step of the dissolution process ensures that you do not overextend yourself by taking a new position or planning to relocate too soon.

6. Make the announcement. You do not want your creditors, customers, and especially your employees to learn that the business is closing from anybody but you. Uncertainty may cost you additional revenues while preparing to close, and disgruntled or deserting employees can hinder your dissolution process. The employee part of this is particularly tricky. If there is cash available, make some provision for your employees. Nothing enrages loyal workers more than the owner closing or selling a business, with a big cash payout, while long-time employees get very little.

7. Work out contracts and obligations that extend beyond your closing date. Negotiate final payments on automobiles, office equipment, and leases. Also inform insurance companies and utility companies of your closing date. Auto and equipment leases are relatively easy matters to fix; if you rent substantial business space, plan this carefully so that you are not paying for unused space for years. This happens all the time. Real estate rental contracts survive many businesses, and someone has to pay (unless the business, of course, is dissolved).

8. Close the business. Terminate production, sales, and services.

9. Dispose of assets. This is also a good time to terminate your business insurance coverage. Some assets can be easily sold, but some are difficult to deal with. Consider donating equipment or other useful items that cannot be sold to charity for a tax deduction. If assets are substantial, especially fixed assets, bring in a broker/dealer to manage the process. The commission is well worth it.

10. Pay off business debts. Prepare final tax returns. This step requires preparing both federal and local tax forms. These forms are more complicated than the annual returns that your business prepares. If your business has not consulted a tax expert prior to dissolution, this is the time to do it.

11. File dissolution papers. Corporations, limited liability companies, limited partnerships, and limited liability partnerships are required to notify the state that they have dissolved. Although a general partnership is not required to register, it is still a good idea to consult your attorney about a way of making your dissolution known to the state.

12. Prepare final forms with the appropriate government bodies. Every agency that registered your business, issued you a license, provided you with tax numbers, or played a role in getting your business up and running should be notified of your dissolution.

13. Close the business bank account.

14. Keep all business records and other business documents for seven years. This will provide you with peace of mind against the event that your business is audited somewhere down the road or some other kind of dispute arises. A disgruntled employee could sue for back wages (whether due or not), or a dispute could arise with final payments on leases.

Simple as that!

Closing a small, part-time business is usually much easier and quicker. It can almost be here today, gone tomorrow. Paying off bills and notifying the state that the business is closed are essential. Obviously, so is the final corporate tax return.

Business Failure

The process listed here is also mostly a workable outline for closing a business of necessity because the business simply is not viable. Some involuntary closings can be handled without filing for bankruptcy. Although the word *bankruptcy* itself conjures up terrible images, it actually can be used effectively to get relief from creditors and possibly to reorganize the business and continue operations after bankruptcy. (Unfortunately, as often happens with small businesses, the bills go away, but the business does too.)

Involuntary closing can be extremely painful, psychologically and financially. Consider the nonfinancial issues first:

loss of self-esteem
explaining to family and friends your business failure
managing employees or others dependent on the business
looking for new employment
sheer complexity of actually closing the business
pressure on family, partners, and investors

The financial issues influence your life for years to come, depending how much you are in debt personally or what resources you used to pay for the business start-up. Here are some of the issues in general:

personal guarantees to the bank or creditors
unresolved tax issues
credit card debt

your home as collateral

money due employees or independent contractors

costs related to bankruptcy

legal bills related to vendor, partner, or investor disputes

Although this book is not about failing as an entrepreneur, it is about being warned how difficult it can be to make a business successful and sustainable and one that actually pays its owners and investors for the risks involved. The topic of bankruptcy is so vast and so complicated that we cannot discuss it in detail. But if hindsight is worth anything, the less you personally are responsible for bills and financial commitments, the better off you will be.

Your primary goal, if you are financing the business yourself or are guaranteeing any financing, or if you offered your home as a security for a loan, is to pay yourself first—that is, get yourself off these loans and conditions just as fast as you can. The business should bear the burden, not the owner. The business can always reorganize or close down or go bankrupt without destroying your credit history and losing you personal assets that took years to acquire. Thus, again and again, you need to be reminded that putting your home as security for a business loan is a very bad idea. If the loan is large, the banker will look for everything—including your pets—to serve as security; your push-back is to let the company bear this burden alone, based on its cash flow and profit potential. But this takes time.

Partners and Investors

Nothing is more stressful than informing partners (many are often silent, not active in the business) and investors that the business is in trouble or is failing. Make sure that you routinely tell all the news to partners and investors if they are not active. They should see, read, and hear from you interpretations of quarterly and annual reports about sales, cash flow, and profitability (or lack thereof of any of these).

A good manager never lies or distorts the facts where money is concerned. In small-business matters, people tend to be trusting. The $20,000 they put in the business may or may not be a large amount of money, but it does not matter. They invested with the expectation that they would get all of it back and then some for their trouble and the degree of risk. It is particularly difficult if your partners and investors are friends or relatives. Troubled business matters can make for some very chilly family dinners.

Most states have Blue Sky laws. Essentially, these laws make entrepreneurs seeking investors qualify the investors as to the amount they will invest and their ability to lose some or all of their investment. A person with $100,000 in total net personal assets would not qualify to invest $50,000 in an uncertain venture, no matter how much he wanted to. But lending and investing goes on all the time among family and friends. As we have discussed, sometimes a promissory note is not even signed, and claims can be conflicting.

If a business fails, you risk losing friends and loss of esteem from family members, but you may also feel an ethical obligation to pay back what was borrowed. This puts an additional burden on you at a time when you are least able to absorb the financial and psychological pressure.

Selling, Merging, or Giving Away a Business

Tiny micro-businesses, like those started and run as part-time from the home, rarely have any real value. They are rarely sold, are not likely to be merged with another business, and probably cannot even be given away. A larger business, seemingly failing but with a few viable years left, could be sold. Likely it is an asset sale; a competitor might want bits and pieces of the company, such as customer lists, patents, copyrights, limited inventory, or a domain name.

Selling a failing business is not easy; most business brokers will not take the listing because they know it will be sold at a huge discount from book value. Since their commission is based on the sale price, they must work as hard (or harder) to sell a failing business as they do a healthy one, but for substantially less commission. Businesses are constantly advertised for sale in regional magazines and the local press and on the Internet. On any one day, there are literally hundreds of thousands of them available, all seeking a new owner. As discussed, many service businesses have no real assets to sell: The local independent meat market is for sale, but all it has is a lease and a few coolers and freezers. All the rest is the goodwill and loyal customers (who can disappear in a minute) when new ownership takes over.

A merger is possible if the business is big enough and there is a ready competitor who is willing to buy it. The competitor's motivation may be to gain some of your company's assets; it also may be willing to take the company to rid itself of a competitor and retire the name. One large book publisher acquired a ten-million-dollar competitor, not for its sales or its copyrights, but simply to make an annoyingly aggressive competitor go away. But even in a merger the competitor is not necessarily willing to take on all of the debt; a merger may solve some of your problems, but the valuation of the company for merger purposes probably will not cover all of your debt. Still, some is better than none, and saving your financial skin, although not completely, could work.

One creative option is to give away a company to someone willing to assume some or all of the debt. Passing along the entire debt is unlikely and rare, but some negotiations to take over, say, past-due vendor accounts for the assets of the company might seem reasonable. It is conceivable that the company could be turned around if the initial start-up debt was not on the books and the new owner only had to pay ongoing expenses. This case is most common with partners, who at this point are probably not on the best of terms anyway.

Epilogue: Final Thoughts

The book ends where it begins: Do you start another business, seek full-time employment, or start up something else part-time and see how it works out? Strangely enough, entrepreneurs, even when they fail, seem never to get enough. Once you have the bug, it is hard to go back to a different lifestyle and work style.

Stories abound about individuals who have failed once, twice, even more times and finally put together a business formula that has made them wealthy beyond their dreams. The irony is, of course, that it took a few tries to work the bugs out. Understanding how businesses fail may be as important as all the up-front planning. Interviewing entrepreneurs who have failed and are now successful can be worthwhile, especially if they are candid about what went wrong.

Business failure, although ultimately about money, is not always caused by insufficient capitalization—although this is often the case. Entrepreneurs take partners with whom they are not well suited; spend money when it should not be spent; make rash decisions without taking the time to understand a problem better. Entrepreneurs are famous for being certain they are right and everyone else is not. They hate to seek advice and dislike even more implementing advice, no matter how worthy it might be. Personal flaws can be masked under the guise of creativity or enthusiasm; poor management brings down many businesses, large and small. Trying to grow too fast, only to find that you have outstripped your capital and human resources, is often the cause of business failure. The best advice is to take your time and build slowly; be conservative financially while keeping your eyes open for new opportunities or a different direction for your business.

Resources

Kansas Business Center

The Kansas Business Center has an excellent outline for business closings: www.kansas.gov/businesscenter/closing/.

St. Louis Small Business Monthly

St. Louis Small Business Monthly addresses going out of business and is another general source for small business information: www.sbmon.com/businessandlaw/tabid/135/itemid/196/default.aspx.

Small-Business Entrepreneur's Checklist

Business Planning and Management Limitations

1. Do you know your own personal management assets and liabilities?

   _____ yes _____ partially _____no

2. Do you have a written small-business plan covering 1 to 5 years?

   _____ yes _____ partially _____no

3. Can you concretely define what product or service you are in?

   _____ yes _____ partially _____no

4. Can you describe in writing what business you are in?

   _____ yes _____ partially _____no

Market Analysis

5. Do you know in detail what factual market conditions and government requirements affect your business?

_____ yes _____ partially _____no

6. Do you know your specific geographic and demographic market areas?

_____ yes _____ partially _____no

7. Do you know your market area business and competitor by name, organization, size, and gross sales?

_____ yes _____ partially _____no

8. Can you describe in writing the strengths and weaknesses of competitors in your defined market areas?

_____ yes _____ partially _____no

Marketing Strategy

9. Can you identify in a written business plan what advantages your products or services have over specific competitors?

_____ yes _____ partially _____no

10. Can you describe in writing how your products and services are distributed or sold?

_____ yes _____ partially _____no

11. Do you know what sources of supplies and costs are required to operate your company?

_____ yes _____ partially _____no

Financial Controls

12. Can you detail the specific monthly cash and credit requirements of your company?

_____ yes _____ partially _____no

13. Do you maintain a file of and stay aware of the advantages of small-business computer planning, accounting, financial management, and marketing controls?

     _____ yes _____ partially _____ no

14. Do you use standard financial industry ratios as a guide to measure your company's annual performance?

     _____ yes _____ partially _____ no

15. Do you maintain written costs of sales, break-even analyses, profit and loss statements, and appropriate accounting journals?

     _____ yes _____ partially _____ no

Personnel Functions

16. Do you know how much personnel money your company spends on human resource development as compared to competitors?

     _____ yes _____ partially _____ no

17. Do you know exactly what employee benefits cost your company?

     _____ yes _____ partially _____ no

18. Do you have a detailed personnel plan for the management staff, clerical, and specific labor (i.e., part-time, union) required to operate your company?

     _____ yes _____ partially _____ no

Operations, Organization, and Special Areas

19. Do you have a detailed building or facility plan that documents the space required to operate the business?

     _____ yes _____ partially _____ no

20. If you have a franchise, do you know why your business is a franchise and the legal limitations or advantages of this business form?

_____ yes _____ partially _____no

21. Do you use specialized consultants on a preplanned basis for accounting, legal, tax, insurance, employee benefits, and other critical business operational areas?

_____ yes _____ partially _____no

Index